A Quick-Start™ Cookbook
COOKING WITH THE OSTER *Countertop* TOASTER OVEN

101 EASY & DELICIOUS RECIPES, PLUS PRO TIPS & ILLUSTRATED INSTRUCTIONS, FROM QUICK-START COOKBOOKS!

BY
TARA ADAMS

QUICK-START COOKBOOKS
SAN FRANCISCO, CA

COPYRIGHT © 2019 Quick-Start Cookbooks

First published 2019

All rights reserved. No part of this book may be reproduced in any form or by any electronic or mechanical means, including information storage and retrieval systems, without permission in writing from the publisher, except by reviewers, who may quote brief passages in a review.

Editor: Quick-Start Cookbooks

Art Direction: Quick-Start Cookbooks

Illustrations: Quick-Start Cookbooks

All photographs in this book © Quick-Start Cookbooks or © Depositphotos.com

Published in the United States of America by Quick-Start Cookbooks
268 Bush St, #3042
San Francisco, CA 94104 USA

www.QuickStartCookbooks.com

Disclaimer:

Oster® is a registered trademark. This book is independently published by Quick-Start Cookbooks, and written to be compatible with the Oster oven. This book is not authorized or endorsed by Oster or its affiliates. Although the publisher and author of this book are practically obsessed with modern cooking techniques, neither represent, nor are associated or affiliated with, any of the brands mentioned in this text.

All content herein represents the author's own experiences and opinions, and do not represent medical or health advice. The responsibility for the consequences of your actions, including your use or misuse of any suggestion or procedure described in this book lies not with the authors, publisher or distributors of this book. We recommend consulting with a licensed health professional before changing your diet or exercise. The author or the publisher does not assume any liability for the use of or inability to use any or all of the information contained in this book, nor does the author or publisher accept responsibility for any type of loss or damage that may be experienced by the user as the result of activities occurring from the use of any information in this book. Use the information responsibly and at your own risk.

The author reserves the right to make changes he or she deems required to future versions of the publication to maintain accuracy.

Reader Reviews

Who knew a humble toaster oven could be used to cook such a variety of recipes! I love this book because it defies the average concept of a toaster oven. Thanks for opening my mind and making me feel so excited about my toaster oven :)

Sonia R

This is one of those high-production, beautiful recipe books that have an interesting take on how to cook. I really love the whole thing, it's exciting and I learned quite a lot from it. The recipes are adventurous, especially for a toaster oven. After trying a few, I became a fan!

Susan A

This book is not your normal toaster book for people who just want mac and cheese. I had no idea what my toaster oven is capable of until I read this book and tried a few recipes. As a college student with no actual kitchen, this book gave me the ability to eat healthy and delicous food and not spend so much on going out.

Rick G

I love the health-minded and almost gourmet attitude of these recipes! I expected typical home toaster oven recipes for quick warm-up type meals, but instead these recipes are a revelation! I used to use my toaster oven to warm up leftovers (I don't like microwaves) and make toast or bake small frozen pastries, but now I use it to make pretty impressive meals. Buy this book, don't look back!

Leslie M.

Terrific collection of unexpected recipes...pretty straightforward instructions. Beautiful book, really nicely presented. It's a pleasure to leaf through and find interesting recipes to try.

Scott B.

Introduction

Start Cooking in Minutes!

The Oster Digital Convection Toaster Oven is the perfect addition to your kitchen because it will allow you maximum flexibility to cook virtually anything you want quickly and easily.

Get the Most Out of Your Oster Toaster Oven!

We're going to teach you how to use your Oster Toaster Oven, but we're also going to go into depth with tips and tricks to get the most out of every cooking experience.

Clear and Illustrated Instructions

This book will make using the Oster Toaster Oven simple and satisfying, so you can start your cooking adventures in minutes.

Go Beyond the Instruction Manual

Learn to make delicious baked goods, as well as perfect breakfasts, lunches, dinners, and so much more.

Independent and Unbiased Recommendations

Gives you all the information you need to choose the best settings and ingredients to make meals that are perfectly tailored to your family. This guide will also teach you ways to avoid common mistakes, so that you can be confident that every dish will come out perfectly.

Amazing Pro Tips

Our pro tips will take you beyond the manual and teach you ways to maximize your cooking for the most perfect results. We're going to take all of the guesswork out of creating dishes that come out perfectly right from the start.

Get a Fast Start with "10 Minute Quick-Start"

Get started in 10 minutes with our handy quick-start guide and you can be cooking right after you take the Oster Toaster Oven out of the box. We cover everything you need to know to get started in minutes.

101 of the Best Recipes on the Planet

We're going to show you how to make a wide variety of delicious meals that are easy to make and sure to be a hit with the whole family.

Contents

ABOUT the Oster Toaster Oven 1

HOW TO USE the Oster Toaster Oven 5

10 Minute Quick-Start 10-11

Pro Tips 13

Breakfast Recipes 17
- Baked Apple Breakfast Oats 18
- Buttery Chocolate Toast 19
- Avocado and Spinach Poached Eggs 21
- Cheesy Baked-Egg Toast 22
- Ham and Cheese Bagel Sandwiches 23
- Ultimate Breakfast Burrito 24
- Peanut Butter & Jelly Banana Boats 25
- Tomatta Spinacha Frittata 26
- Toasted Cinnamon Bananas 28
- Ultimate Breakfast Sandwich 29

Lunch Recipes 31
- Balsamic Roasted Chicken 32
- Rolled Salmon Sandwich 33
- Chicken Caprese Sandwich 34
- Easy Prosciutto Grilled Cheese 35
- Herb-Roasted Chicken Tenders 36
- Moroccan Pork Kebabs 37
- Roasted Mini Peppers 38
- Pecan Crunch Catfish and Asparagus 40
- Parmesan-Crusted Pork Loin 41
- Persimmon Toast with Sour Cream & Cinnamon 42
- Roasted Beet Salad with Oranges & Beet Greens 43
- Roasted Grape and Goat Cheese Crostinis 44

- Roasted Delicata Squash with Kale 45
- Skinny Black Bean Flautas 47
- Turkey-Stuffed Peppers 48
- Spice-Roasted Almonds 49
- Spiralized Parsnip and Sweet Potato Latkes 50
- Sweet Potato Chips 51
- Country Comfort Corn Bread 52
- Perfect Size French Fries 53
- Portobello Pesto Burgers 54
- Parmigiano Reggiano and Prosciutto Toasts with Balsamic Glaze 56
- Philly Cheesesteak Egg Rolls 57
- Seven-Layer Tostadas 58
- Roasted-Fennel Ditalini and Shrimp 59
- Spicy Avocado Cauliflower Toast 60
- Squash and Zucchini Mini Pizza 61
- Basic Roasted Tofu 63
- Butter Fish with Sake and Miso 64
- Chicken Breast with Rosemary 65
- Dijon and Swiss Croque Monsieur 66
- Kalamata Mozarella Pita Melts 67
- Tomato Avocado Melt 68
- Vegetarian Philly Sandwich 69

Dinner Recipes 71

- Baked Veggie Egg Rolls.. 72
- Broccoli and Avocado Tacos... 73
- Broiled Tilapia with Parmesan and Herbs................................. 74
- Coconut-Crusted Haddock with Curried Pumpkin Seeds 75
- Tex-Mex Chicken Quesadillas.. 77
- Oven-Fried Herbed Chicken... 78
- Miso-Glazed Salmon.. 79
- Pesto & White Wine Salmon.. 80
- Rigatoni with Roasted Broccoli and Chick Peas..................... 81
- Mozzarella & Olive Pizza Bagels.. 82
- Roasted Butternut Squash with Brussels Sprouts & Sweet Potato Noodles....84
- Spicy Sesame-Honey Chicken... 85
- Fennel & Tomato Chicken Paillard... 86
- Traditional English Fish and Chips.. 87
- Cheddar & Dijon Tuna Melt.. 88
- Adobo Turkey Chimichangas... 89

Sides 91

- Avocado, Tomato, & Grape Salad with Crunchy Potato Croutons..... 92
- Baked Parmesan Zucchini.. 93
- Garlic & Parmesan Bread Bites... 94
- Roasted Garlic Fries... 95
- Roasted Brussels Sprouts.. 97
- Green Mango Salad.. 98
- Honey-Roasted Carrots with Sesame Seeds.......................... 99
- Lemon-Garlic Kale Salad.. 100
- Lemon-Thyme Bruschetta.. 101

- Simple Roasted Asparagus.. 102
- Roasted Beets with Grapefruit Glaze..................................... 103
- Rosemary & Thyme Roasted Fingerling Potatoes................. 104
- Roasted Curried Cauliflower.. 106
- Roasted Radishes with Brown Butter, Lemon, and Radish Tops....107
- Garlic & Olive Oil Spring Vegetables..................................... 108
- Garlic Herb Tomatoes.. 109
- Roasted Vegetable and Kale Salad.. 110
- Traditional Greek Spanakopita... 111

Snacks 113

- Baked Avocados with Strawberry Salsa................................ 114
- Baked Eggs with Marinara and Parmesan............................. 115
- Easy & Quick Bread Pudding... 116
- Twice-Baked Sweet Potato with Coconut.............................. 117
- Zucchini Lasagna Toasts.. 118
- Mushroom Onion Strudel... 119
- Simply Delicious Garlic Kale Chips....................................... 120
- Nacho Avocado Toast... 122
- Parmesan Green Onion Hash Brown Cups........................... 123
- Wholesome Pita Chips... 124
- Tomato Whole Grain Grilled Cheese Bites............................ 125

Desserts....................................... 127

- Oatmeal Raisin Cookies... 128
- Cinnamon Apple Tart.. 129
- Blackberry Peach (or Apple) Cobbler.................................... 131
- Blueberry Cream Cheese Croissant Puff............................... 132
- Peanut Butter & Jelly Bars... 133
- Peanut Butter Cookies... 134
- Cinnamon Pear Oatmeal Crisp... 136
- Buttery Plum Clafoutis... 137
- Single-Serving Chocolate Chip Cookies................................ 139
- Oatmeal Cookie Peach Cobbler... 140
- Strawberry Chocolate Chip Banana Bread Bars................... 141

CHAPTER 1

About the Oster Toaster Oven

What Does It Do?

I know what you're thinking... Isn't a toaster oven just a miniature oven? In some ways, yes, but the features and benefits of the Oster Convection Toaster Oven really set it apart from conventional ovens as well as other toaster ovens. The Oster Toaster Oven features advanced digital controls allowing you maximum flexibility and accuracy, but it also harnesses the power of convection cooking for faster, more even cooking. And because it features a large cooking space, you are able to cook a wide variety of different dishes without having to turn on your regular oven.

What Does It NOT Do?

The Oster Toaster Oven is a marvel of functionality. From convection cooking to perfect defrosting, it does so many things. But there are a few things it can't do. The Oster Toaster Oven will not take the place of your microwave because it will not heat up food as quickly. It does, however, heat up much faster than a conventional oven. You are also somewhat limited by the size of the Oster Toaster Oven. While it does feature a large cooking compartment, you will not be able to cook a twenty pound turkey in it. Other than these few limitations, the Oster Toaster Oven will handle most of your cooking needs.

Who Is It Good For?

Because the Oster Toaster Oven is so versatile and easy to use, it is good for practically anyone. Families who want the flexibility to cook small meals and snacks will love how simple it is to use. And if you happen to be cooking large meals for holidays, like Thanksgiving, the Oster Toaster Oven is a great way to free up space in your regular oven, or keep things warm until dinnertime. The Oster Toaster Oven is also perfect for college students and singles who often need to cook quick meals for one. Instead of preheating your large regular oven, the Oster Toaster Oven heats in seconds and is specifically designed to handle small meals. It also allows you to easily defrost items, saving you time.

Perfect for the Whole Family

The Oster Toaster Oven is a great alternative to a conventional oven because it offers greater flexibility, so everyone in the family can use it. Because you often only need to make small meals or snacks, your regular oven can be inefficient. First of all, a regular oven takes time to heat up. The Oster Toaster Oven, on the other hand, heats up in just a fraction of the time so you can get cooking right away. The Oster Toaster Oven's easy-to-use digital controls also take a lot of the guesswork out of cooking. Therefore, you don't have to be a professional chef to easily make meals that are sure to please. The Oster Toaster Oven is also perfect for those times when the family is making a really big meal and there just isn't enough space in the regular oven.

Who Is It NOT Good For?

While the Oster Toaster Oven is perfect for nearly any situation, if you have limited space in your kitchen and do not need another cooking appliance, the Oster Toaster Oven may not be for you. If your family prefers to only make large meals, the small size of the Oster Toaster Oven may not be large enough to meet your needs.

A Few Cautions

As with any cooking appliance with a heating element, you will want to exercise caution when operating the Oster Toaster Oven. Always make sure the oven is placed on a stable and level surface and that children are properly supervised while using it. When removing items from the oven, always be sure to wear oven mitts and use the side handles to move the oven when hot. When opening the door to the oven, make sure your face is a safe distance, as the oven will be very hot after cooking. Before cleaning the trays or inner surfaces of the oven, make sure it has fully cooled after cooking. And of course, make sure to turn the oven off as soon has you have finished cooking.

Health Benefits

One of the main issues facing families these days is overconsuming processed foods and fast food, which are often high in fat, sugars, and preservatives. And one of the best ways to deal with this is to learn to cook healthy meals at home. But the problem is that cooking at home can be time consuming and involves a lot of equipment. That's where your Oster Toaster Oven comes in. Because it is so easy to use and clean, cooking at home is no longer a hassle. The Oster Toaster Oven features easy-to-use controls and convection cooking, so even a beginner can become an expert home chef in no time. Once you've gotten the hang of how it works, the whole family will want to join in the fun of cooking fast, easy, and most importantly, healthy meals.

A Brief History of Toaster Ovens

Believe it or not, the toaster oven actually predates the pop-up toaster by about nine years. The first toaster oven was produced in 1910 by the Westinghouse Company as a way to incorporate most of the functions of a traditional oven but in a much smaller package. The pop-up toaster we're all familiar with didn't come along until 1919. Over the years, features were added to toaster ovens to give them more flexibility and function. Most notably, we saw toaster ovens designed with settings for different types of food. Eventually, features like convection were added and allowed users to cook virtually anything in their toaster ovens... as long as it was small enough.

CHAPTER 2

How to Use the Oster Toaster Oven

Setting Up Your Toaster Oven

Your toaster oven really couldn't be easier to use. The front door allows you access to the racks, which slide in and out to provide easy access to your food before, during, and after cooking.

Once you have removed the toaster oven from the box, place it on a level surface near a grounded power outlet. Plug the toaster oven in and remove the trays from the oven. Before using, make sure to thoroughly clean the trays with soap and water. You are now set up and ready to start using your Oster Toaster Oven.

Learning the controls

The great thing about the Oster Toaster Oven is that all of the controls are labeled for easy use. You don't have to bother with confusing dials. Let's take a look at how the Oster Toaster Oven works.

❶ 1 Temperature Control Knob: This controls the oven temperature. Simply turn clockwise to set the oven to any temperature between 0°F to 450°F.

❷ 2 Function Selector Knob: This controls HOW the temperature you selected above is achieved. Depending on which function you select (Warm, Broil, Bake, Toast, Turbo), and which temperature you've selected, the oven will turn on/off its heating elements and air circulation. Refer to the recipe for which function mode to select.

❸ 3 Timer Control Knob with Bell Signal: This knob is basically an "on" button with a timer built-in. The oven will turn off when the timer runs out and you'll hear its bell go "ding!".

❹ 4 Removeable Crumb Tray: This tray is at the bottom, under the heating elements. It pulls out for easy cleaning.

❺ 5 Baking Pan & Cookie Sheet: Use this for baking.

❻ 6 Removeable Wire Rack: Use this for broiling and grilling. You can place it in two positions to get closer or further from the above heating elements.

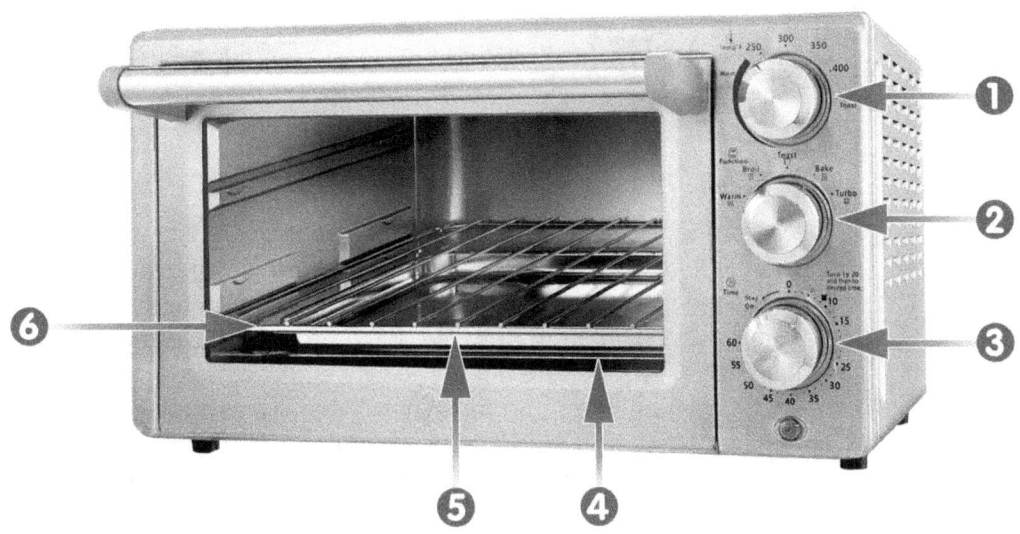

The cooking process

The Oster Toaster Oven is one of the most advanced toaster ovens on the planet due to its digital controls and user-friendly design. But perhaps the best feature of the Oster Toaster Oven is its ability to cook using convection. Unlike regular baking, convection produces the most even heat possible by circulating the heated air. It's perfect for many different types of cooking when you want your food to be evenly cooked throughout. It's also a great way to ensure amazing results when baking.

From the moment you choose your cooking program, the Oster Toaster Oven begins heating quickly. A great feature of this oven is that is preheats so quickly. And unlike many competing toaster ovens, the Oster allows you to cook up to 450°F, which allows you to cook many foods you would not be able to cook in other toaster ovens. When you're finished cooking, the timer will go off and the oven will automatically turn itself off. That's not just a great way to save energy, it's also an important safety feature. After the oven has had a chance to cool, you can clean it using a damp cloth or sponge to remove any spatter that may have occurred during the cooking process.

Workarounds

We've already explored many of the things your Oster Toaster Oven can do, so now let's talk a little about problem solving. When you're cooking in a conventional oven, it is pretty common to line your baking sheets with aluminum foil. It's a great way to keep those baking trays from getting dirty, and that's pretty helpful after your meal. But using aluminum foil in the Oster Toaster Oven is not a good idea. The problem is that using aluminum foil in the Oster Toaster Oven can cause the oven to get too hot - sometimes over 500°F, and a toaster oven, unlike your conventional oven, isn't designed to safely work at such a high temperature. To combat this problem and still have a way to line the trays of your toaster oven, try using parchment paper. It will keep food from sticking to the trays, and you can just throw it out after cooking.

You may have noticed that the Oster Toaster Oven features a large cooking space inside the oven. As a result, you can cook more efficiently by cooking on several levels at once. While only one cooking rack is included with the oven, you can purchase additional racks. Just make sure to purchase racks in the correct size.

Often, you will see packaged foods with a different temperature recommendation for cooking food in toaster ovens. However, because the Oster Toaster Oven cooks almost exactly like a regular oven, it is usually not necessary to use the recommended toaster oven temperature setting. Doing this may actually cause your food to come out overcooked. We suggest that you reduce all toaster oven temperature recommendations by twenty-five degrees to avoid overcooking.

10 Minute Quick-Start

Your Oster Toaster Oven is perfect for cooking all kinds of meals from breakfast to dessert, and amazing snacks, too. And of course, it also makes great toast. But for our first meal, let's start with something that is a complete meal, but also a great way to start your day. We're going to start with the ultimate breakfast sandwich.

1 Collect These Ingredients:

- 2 English muffins
- 2 eggs
- 2 slices American or Cheddar cheese
- 2 pork sausage patties or 4 slices bacon
- 1 tablespoon butter, softened

2 Collect These Tools:

- Bread knife
- Non-stick baking tray
- Spatula

The goal of the "10 Minute Quick-Start" is to walk you through making your first meal so you "learn by doing" in under 10 minutes. Once you've had a chance to become familiar with how your Oster Toaster Oven works, you can begin experimenting with all different types of foods.

3 Follow These Steps:

1. Start by setting the toaster oven to Toast and warming up a non-stick pan.
2. Add sausages or bacon to pan and butter the insides of the muffins.
3. While the sausages cook, put the muffins in the toaster oven to toast until crispy brown, about 5–7 minutes.
4. Set the sausages aside and add eggs to the skillet.
5. Let the whites set, then carefully flip the eggs to keep the yolk intact.
6. Turn off the heat and add cheese and sausage to the top of the egg. This will allow everything to melt together but leave the yolk with the perfect consistency.
7. Add the mixture to the muffin and enjoy the perfect breakfast.

Congratulations!

You've just made your first meal with your Oster Toaster Oven. Now that you've gotten the hang of the basics, it's time to start experimenting with everything your Oster Toaster Oven can do. Once you've been using it for a while, you will wonder how you ever lived without it.

CHAPTER 3

Pro Tips

The Best Way to Defrost

Defrosting food items can be a challenge, and defrosting incorrectly can lead to unfortunate results. Ideally, the best way to defrost your food is gradually and evenly so that all of the food defrosts at the same rate and to the same temperature. This is the best way to ensure even cooking. Unfortunately, many methods for defrosting result in uneven temperatures, but your Oster Toaster Oven can help solve this problem. While using a microwave is the most common choice for quick defrosting, microwaves are also notorious for not heating food evenly. This can lead to one part of the food being partially cooked, while another part is still frozen. The Oster Toaster Oven features a specific defrost function that controls a low level of heat and circulates the air for even coverage. This way, your food will defrost quickly, but it will be evenly defrosted and ready to cook using your preferred method.

Use a Pizza Stone

Your Oster Toaster Oven features a large cooking compartment, and this is helpful for many different reasons. One of the most commonly cooked items in toaster ovens is pizza, and while you can certainly use it to heat up a frozen pizza, you can also make amazing homemade pizzas right in your Oster Toaster Oven. If you want to take your pizza game to the next level, it's time to start cooking the way the pros do: with a pizza stone. While pizza may seem simple- crust, sauce, cheese, toppings- it's actually a very mysterious dish because none of these ingredients cook at the same rate. This has led chefs to look for ways to even out the cooking process for better results. The most common pizza problem is that the cheese melts and browns faster than the dough bakes. This results in a problem you may have experienced: perfectly melted cheese, and a raw, doughy crust. Then you keep cooking and end up with perfectly baked crust and burned cheese. The easiest way to fix this is by using a pizza stone, and because your Oster Toaster Oven features a large cooking compartment, it can accommodate a pizza stone that is twelve inches in diameter. Once you've purchased a pizza stone, place it in the oven and turn on the heat to bake at the highest temperature. In order to function properly, the stone needs to heat up in the oven for at least thirty minutes. This will allow the stone to retain heat so that when you place your pizza on it, the crust will start cooking quickly. This will help you achieve a nicely-baked crust with perfectly melted cheese.

Better Baking with Silpat

One of the most common problems people encounter when baking is cookies sticking to baking sheets, or burned bottoms. Even with even heat, it is still possible to end up with cookies that are just not evenly cooked. The best way to deal with this problem is to use a revolutionary product called Silpat. They're widely available and are made with a combination of high-strength silicon and a heat-safe mesh that encourages even cooking. Silicon has amazing non-stick properties, so anything you put on them will come off with ease. Simply line your cooking trays with Silpat liners and place your food items directly on the Silpat. There is no need to grease or butter them, and they can withstand very high heat. Once it has finished cooking, your food should slide effortlessly off the Silpat liners, and the bottoms should be evenly cooked.

Broil Instead of Grilling

Let's face it, who doesn't love perfectly char-grilled food? But if you don't need to cook a lot of food at once, grilling can be inefficient, dirty, and not great for your health. A great alternative to grilling is broiling, which uses a high heat element to easily and safely char your food. The Oster Toaster Oven features a high powered broiler, and because the oven is so adjustable, you have a lot of control over how close your food is to the broiling element. In order to get started broiling, place your food item on the broiling tray and slide the tray into the oven. In order to get a little extra char on your food, such as a burger or steak, brush the top with a small amount of canola oil or butter. Set the oven to broil and watch as your food is perfectly charred. Because of the high heat produced by the Oster Toaster Oven, you can achieve a perfectly medium-rare steak or burger and still have a nicely charred exterior. This is a great way to enjoy grilled foods in bad weather or during the winter.

Avoid Overcooking

While you may be familiar with cooking in a conventional oven, a toaster oven works a little bit differently. First of all, it's much smaller, which means two things: it heats up a lot faster, and it retains heat very well. As a result, many users find that if they follow the temperature and time settings for dishes meant to be cooked in conventional ovens, they find that their food has overcooked. Many toaster ovens also include a convection feature, which will also affect cooking times. On the regular setting, plan to check your food about five minutes before the recipe says is the normal cooking time. For convection cooking, reduce the overall cooking time by 20%. Once you get a feel for how your oven works, you will become more comfortable with how long cooking takes, but at first, these guidelines should help avoid overcooking.

CHAPTER 4

Breakfast Recipes

Baked Apple
Breakfast Oats

This recipe is super simple, but so delicious. With only a few ingredients, it is a great way to throw together a quick breakfast in a hurry.

Servings: 1
Prep Time: 15 Minutes
Cook Time: 15 Minutes

1/3 cup vanilla Greek yogurt
1/3 cup rolled oats
1 apple
1 tablespoon peanut butter

1. Preheat your toaster oven to 400°F and set it on the warm setting.
2. Cut your apples into chunks approximately 1/2-inch-thick.
3. Place apples on an oven-safe dish with some space between each chunk and sprinkle with cinnamon.
4. Bake in the oven for 12 minutes.
5. Combine yogurt and oats in a bowl.
6. Remove the apples from the oven and combine with the yogurt.
7. Top with peanut butter and you have a delicious and high-protein breakfast.

Nutrition
Calories: 350, Sodium: 134 mg, Dietary Fiber: 8.1 g, Total Fat: 11.2 g, Total Carbs: 52.5 g, Protein: 12.7 g.

Buttery Chocolate Toast

It may be simple, but that doesn't stop it from being delicious. Make this magnificent take on toast in only a few minutes.

Servings: 1
Prep Time: 5 Minutes
Cook Time: 5 Minutes

1. Start by toasting the bread in your toaster oven.
2. Spread the coconut oil over the toast.
3. Drizzle maple syrup in lines over the toast.
4. Sprinkle cacao powder and serve.

Whole wheat bread slices
Coconut oil
Pure maple syrup
Cacao powder

Nutrition

Calories: 101, Sodium: 133 mg, Dietary Fiber: 2.4 g, Total Fat: 3.5 g, Total Carbs: 14.8 g, Protein: 4.0 g.

Avocado and Spinach
Poached Eggs

Even the name is mouth-watering. This recipe is simple to cook and doesn't have any adventurous ingredients, yet the finished product seems like it came right out of a chef's kitchen.

Servings: 1
Prep Time: 7 Minutes
Cook Time: 10 Minutes

2 eggs
1/2 avocado
2 slices bruschetta
1 bunch spinach
1 pinch salt
1 pinch pepper

1. Start by preheating the toaster oven to 400°F.
2. Bring a pan of water to a rolling boil.
3. Place your bruschetta on a pan and toast it in the oven for 10 minutes.
4. Once the water is boiling, whisk it around in a circle until it creates a vortex.
5. Drop one egg in the hole and turn the heat to low, then poach for 2 minutes.
6. Repeat with the second egg.
7. Mash the avocado and spread it over the toast while your eggs poach.
8. Add the eggs to the toast and top with spinach.

Nutrition

Calories: 409, Sodium: 553 mg, Dietary Fiber: 14.2 g, Total Fat: 29.7 g, Total Carbs: 21.7 g, Protein: 22.7 g.

Cheesy Baked-Egg Toast

Just the name sounds delicious, but wait until you see the finished product. This is one of my favorite breakfast meals, hands down.

Servings: 4
Prep Time: 10 Minutes
Cook Time: 10 Minutes

4 slices wheat bread
4 eggs
1 cup shredded cheese
2 tablespoons softened butter

1. Start by preheating your toaster oven to 350°F.
2. Place your bread on a greased baking sheet.
3. Use a teaspoon to push a square into the bread creating a little bed for the egg.
4. Sprinkle salt and pepper over the bread.
5. Break one egg into each square. Spread butter over each edge of the bread.
6. Sprinkle 1/4 cup cheese over buttered area.
7. Bake for 10 minutes or until the egg is solid and the cheese is golden brown.

Nutrition

Calories: 297, Sodium: 410 mg, Dietary Fiber: 1.9 g, Total Fat: 20.4 g, Total Carbs: 12.3 g, Protein: 16.3 g.

Ham and Cheese
Bagel Sandwiches

These sandwiches are the perfect meal to cook fast and take on the go. It doesn't hurt that they taste as spectacular as they look.

Servings: 2
Prep Time: 5 Minutes
Cook Time: 5 Minutes

2 bagels
4 teaspoons honey mustard
4 slices cooked honey ham
4 slices Swiss cheese

1. Start by preheating your toaster oven to 400°F.
2. Spread honey mustard on each half of the bagel.
3. Add ham and cheese and close the bagel.
4. Bake the sandwich until the cheese is fully melted, it should take about 5 minutes.

Nutrition

Calories: 588, Sodium: 1450 mg, Dietary Fiber: 2.3 g, Total Fat: 20.1 g, Total Carbs: 62.9 g, Protein: 38.4 g.

Ultimate Breakfast Burrito

The breakfast burrito is an awesome invention because it allows you to take your breakfast on the go, and this recipe is fantastic because it takes the breakfast burrito and makes it even better.

Servings: 8
Prep Time: 20 Minutes
Cook Time:: 20 Minute

- 16 ounces cooked bacon ends and pieces
- 16 eggs
- 1 tablespoon butter
- 8 hash brownsquares
- 8 large soft flour tortillas
- 2 diced jalapenos
- 2 cups shredded sharp cheddar

1. Place bacon on a baking sheet in your toaster oven. Bake it at 450°F until it reaches your desired level of crispiness and set aside.
2. Whisk together eggs in a bowl and set aside.
3. Melt butter into a sauce pan and mix in your eggs until they are starting to cook but not fully hardened.
4. While your eggs are cooking, microwave and cool your hash brown squares.
5. Roll out your tortillas and top them with hash browns, bacon, jalapenos, and cheese.
6. Wrap up the burritos and place them seam-down on a baking sheet.
7. Bake at 375 for 15–20 minutes.

Nutrition

Calories: 698, Sodium: 1821 mg, Dietary Fiber: 3.4 g, Total Fat: 43.7 g, Total Carbs: 32.9 g, Protein: 42.1 g.

Peanut Butter & Jelly
Banana Boats

This recipe is great for a fun breakfast packed with everything you need to start the day, or a mid-day snack to keep the energy up.

Servings: 1
Prep Time: 5 Minutes
Cook Time: 15 Minutes

1 banana
1/4 cup peanut butter
1/4 cup jelly
1 tablespoon granola

1. Start by preheating your toaster oven to 350°F.
2. Slice the banana lengthwise and separate slightly.
3. Spread peanut butter and jelly in the gap.
4. Sprinkle granola over the entire banana.
5. Bake for 15 minutes.

Nutrition
Calories: 724, Sodium: 327 mg, Dietary Fiber: 9.2 g, Total Fat: 36.6 g, Total Carbs: 102.9 g, Protein: 20.0 g.

Tomatta Spinacha Frittata

The only thing more fun than saying the word "frittata" is eating one. This recipe creates a whole meal in a single dish and is a great way to start off a parade of amazing toaster oven recipes.

Servings: 4
Prep Time: 15 Minutes
Cook Time: 30 Minutes

3 tablespoons olive oil
10 large eggs
2 teaspoons kosher salt
1/2 teaspoon black pepper
1 (5-ounce) bag baby spinach
1 pint grape tomatoes
4 scallions
8 ounces feta cheese

1. Preheat your toaster oven to 350°F.
2. Halve your tomatoes and slice your scallions into thin pieces.
3. Add oil to a 2-quart oven-safe pan, making sure to brush it on the sides of the dish as well as the bottom. Place the dish in your toaster oven.
4. Combine the eggs, salt, and pepper in a medium mixing bowl and whisk together for a minute.
5. Add spinach, tomatoes, and scallions to the bowl and mix together until even.
6. Crumble feta cheese into the bowl and mix together gently. Remove the dish from the oven and pour in the egg mixture.
7. Put the dish back into the oven and bake for 25–30 minutes, or until the edges of the frittata are browned.

Nutrition

Calories: 448, Sodium: 515 mg, Dietary Fiber: 2.3 g, Total Fat: 35.4 g, Total Carbs: 9.3 g, Protein: 25.9 g.

Toasted Cinnamon Bananas

These may not be great to look at, but they are another simple recipe bursting with flavor.

Servings: 1
Prep Time: 10 Minutes
Cook Time: 10 Minutes

1 ripe banana
Lemon juice
2 teaspoons honey
Ground cinnamon

1. Start by preheating the toaster oven to 350°F.
2. Slice the bananas lengthwise and place them on a greased baking sheet.
3. Brush each slice with lemon juice.
4. Drizzle honey and sprinkle cinnamon over each slice.
5. Bake for 10 minutes.

Nutrition
Calories: 154, Sodium: 3 mg, Dietary Fiber: 4.2 g, Total Fat: 0.5 g, Total Carbs: 40.2 g, Protein: 1.5 g.

Ultimate Breakfast Sandwich

Pardon the pun, but breakfast is my jam, and there are few breakfast items I enjoy more than a good breakfast sandwich. And the only thing better than a good breakfast sandwich is an ultimate breakfast sandwich.

Servings: 2
Prep Time: 5 Minutes
Cook Time: 5 Minutes

2 English muffins
2 eggs
2 slices aged yellow cheddar
2 large spicy pork sausage patties
Softened butter

1. Start by setting the toaster oven to toast and warming up a non-stick pan.
2. Add sausages to pan and butter the insides of the muffins.
3. While the sausages cook, put the muffins in the toaster oven to toast until crispy brown, about 5–7 minutes.
4. Set the sausages aside and add eggs to the skillet.
5. Let the whites set, then carefully flip the eggs to keep the yolks intact.
6. Turn off the heat and add cheese and sausage to the top of the egg. This will allow everything to melt together but leave the yolks with the perfect consistency.
7. Add the mixture to the muffin and enjoy the perfect breakfast.

Nutrition

Calories: 332, Sodium: 677 mg, Dietary Fiber: 2.0 g, Total Fat: 14.9 g, Total Carbs: 26.1 g, Protein: 22.7 g.

CHAPTER 5

Lunch Recipes

Balsamic Roasted Chicken

It doesn't get more gourmet than this; and guess what? All you need is a toaster oven to bake some amazing chicken.

Servings: 4
Prep Time: 10 Minutes + Marinade Time
Cook Time: 1 Hour

1/2 cup balsamic vinegar
1/4 cup Dijon mustard
1/3 cup olive oil
Juice and zest from 1 lemon
3 minced garlic cloves
1 teaspoon salt
1 teaspoon pepper
4 bone-in, skin-on chicken thighs
4 bone-in, skin-on chicken drumsticks
1 tablespoon chopped parsley

1. Mix vinegar, lemon juice, mustard, olive oil, garlic, salt, and pepper in a bowl, then pour into a sauce pan.
2. Roll chicken pieces in the pan, then cover and marinate for at least 2 hours, but up to 24 hours.
3. Preheat the toaster oven to 400°F and place the chicken on a fresh baking sheet, keeping the marinade for later.
4. Roast the chicken for 50 minutes.
5. Remove the chicken and cover it with foil to keep it warm. Place the marinade in the toaster oven for about 5 minutes until it simmers down and begins to thicken.
6. Pour marinade over chicken and sprinkle with parsley and lemon zest.

Nutrition

Calories: 1537, Sodium: 1383 mg, Dietary Fiber: 0.8 g, Total Fat: 70.5 g, Total Carbs: 2.4 g, Protein: 210.4 g.

Rolled Salmon Sandwich

I am not often a fan of fish in any form, but when it tastes like this you'll forget it is fish at all. What a great way to get those important omega-3s into your diet.

Servings: 1
Prep Time: 5 Minutes
Cook Time: 5 Minutes

1 piece of flatbread
1 salmon filet
Pinch of salt
1 tablespoon green onion, chopped
1/4 teaspoon dried sumac
1/2 teaspoon thyme
1/2 teaspoon sesame seeds
1/4 English cucumber
1 tablespoon yogurt

1. Start by peeling and chopping the cucumber. Cut the salmon at a 45-degree angle into 4 slices and lay them flat on the flatbread.
2. Sprinkle salmon with salt to taste. Sprinkle onions, thyme, sumac, and sesame seeds evenly over the salmon.
3. Broil the salmon for at least 3 minutes, but more if you want a more well-done fish.
4. While you broil your salmon, mix together the yogurt and cucumber. Remove your flatbread from the toaster oven and put it on a plate, then spoon the yogurt mix over the salmon.
5. Fold the sides of the flatbread in and roll it up for a gourmet lunch that you can take on the go.

Nutrition

Calories: 347, Sodium: 397 mg, Dietary Fiber: 1.6 g, Total Fat: 12.4 g, Total Carbs: 20.6 g, Protein: 38.9 g.

Chicken Caprese Sandwich

The name sounds a little fancy, and believe me the sandwich is out-of-this-world good, but the truth is it is pretty simple - which is great when you are looking for something tasty, but you're short on time.

Servings: 2
Prep Time: 3 Minutes
Cook Time: 3 Minutes

2 leftover chicken breasts, or pre-cooked breaded chicken
1 large ripe tomato
4 ounces mozzarella cheese slices
4 slices of whole grain bread
1/4 cup olive oil
1/3 cup fresh basil leaves
Salt and pepper to taste

1. Start by slicing your tomatoes into thin slices.
2. Layer tomatoes then cheese over two slice of bread and place on a greased baking sheet.
3. Toast in the toaster oven for about 2 minutes or until the cheese is melted.
4. Heat your chicken while the cheese melts.
5. Remove from oven, sprinkle with basil, and add chicken.
6. Drizzle with oil and add salt and pepper.
7. Top with other slice of bread and serve.

Nutrition

Calories: 808, Sodium: 847 mg, Dietary Fiber: 5.2 g, Total Fat: 43.6 g, Total Carbs: 30.7 g, Protein: 78.4 g.

Easy Prosciutto
Grilled Cheese

Who says that grilled cheese can't be an adult food? This recipe takes grilled cheese to a whole new level, a level that your taste buds won't soon forget.

Servings: 1
Prep Time: 5 Minutes
Cook Time: 5 Minutes

2 slices of muenster cheese
2 slices of white bread
Four thinly-shaved pieces of prosciutto
1 tablespoon sweet and spicy pickles

1. Set your oven on the toast setting.
2. Place your bread flat and put one slice of cheese on each piece of bread.
3. Put prosciutto on one slice and pickles on the other.
4. Transfer to a baking sheet and toast for 4 minutes or until the cheese is melted.
5. Combine both sides, cut, and serve.

Nutrition

Calories: 460, Sodium: 2180 mg, Dietary Fiber: 0 g, Total Fat: 25.2 g, Total Carbs: 11.9 g, Protein: 44.2 g.

Herb-Roasted Chicken Tenders

This recipe takes a kid's staple and gives it a little adult flair; your kids will still love them, but you won't need to scramble to find something else to eat.

Servings: 2
Prep Time: 5 Minutes
Cook Time: 10 Minutes

7 ounces chicken tenders
1 tablespoon olive oil
1/2 teaspoon Herbes de Provence
2 tablespoons Dijon mustard
1 tablespoon honey
Salt and pepper

1. Start by preheating your toaster oven to 450°F.
2. Brush the bottom of a pan with 1/2 tablespoon olive oil.
3. Season the chicken with herbs, salt, and pepper.
4. Place the chicken in a single flat layer in the pan and drizzle the remaining olive oil over it.
5. Bake for about 10 minutes.
6. While the chicken is baking mix together the mustard and honey for a nice sauce on the side.

Nutrition
Calories: 297, Sodium: 268 mg, Dietary Fiber: 0.8 g, Total Fat: 15.5 g, Total Carbs: 9.6 g, Protein: 29.8 g.

Moroccan Pork Kebabs

I have a busy life with a busy family so I usually like to keep my recipes simple. This one is a little heavy on the ingredients side, but it is so worth it in the end.

Servings: 4
Prep Time: 40 Minutes
Cook Time: 45 Minutes

- 1/4 cup orange juice
- 1 tablespoon tomato paste
- 1 clove chopped garlic
- 1 tablespoon ground cumin
- 1/8 teaspoon ground cinnamon
- 4 tablespoons olive oil
- 1 1/2 teaspoons salt
- 3/4 teaspoon black pepper
- 1 1/2 pounds boneless pork loin
- 1 small eggplant
- 1 small red onion
- Pita bread (optional)
- 1/2 small cucumber
- 2 tablespoons chopped fresh mint
- Wooden skewers

1. Start by placing the wooden skewers in water to soak.
2. Cut pork loin and eggplant into 1 to 1 1/2-inch chunks.
3. Preheat your toaster oven to 425°F.
4. Cut cucumber and onions into pieces and chop the mint.
5. In a large bowl, combine the orange juice, tomato paste, garlic, cumin, cinnamon, 2 tablespoons of oil, 1 teaspoon of salt, and 1/2 teaspoon of pepper.
6. Mix in the pork and refrigerate for at least 30 minutes, but up to 8 hours.
7. Mix together vegetables, remaining oil, and salt and pepper.
8. Skewer the vegetables and bake them for 20 minutes.
9. Add the pork to the skewers and bake for an additional 25 minutes.
10. Remove ingredients from skewer and sprinkle with mint, serve with flatbread if using.

Nutrition

Calories: 465, Sodium: 1061 mg, Dietary Fiber: 5.6 g, Total Fat: 20.8 g, Total Carbs: 21.9 g, Protein: 48.2 g.

Roasted Mini Peppers

If you love peppers, then you will eat these things like they are candy. They are super simple to roast and about as healthy a snack as you can get.

Servings: 6
Prep Time: 2 Minutes
Cook Time: 15 Minutes

1 bag mini bell peppers
Cooking spray
Salt and pepper to taste

1. Start by preheating your toaster oven to 400°F.
2. Wash and dry the peppers then place them flat on a baking sheet.
3. Spray them with cooking spray and sprinkle with salt and pepper.
4. Roast for 15 minutes.

Nutrition
Calories: 19, Sodium: 2 mg, Dietary Fiber: 1.3 g, Total Fat: 0.3 g, Total Carbs: 3.6 g, Protein: 0.6 g.

Pecan Crunch
Catfish and Asparagus

Those who say that catfish isn't edible just don't know how to prepare it. This recipe offers taste and texture that accent the unique flavor of catfish.

Servings: 4
Prep Time: 5 minutes
Cook Time: 12 Minutes

- 1 cup whole wheat panko breadcrumbs
- 1/4 cup chopped pecans
- 3 teaspoons chopped fresh thyme
- 1 1/2 tablespoons extra-virgin olive oil, plus more for the pan
- Salt and pepper to taste
- 1 1/4 pounds asparagus
- 1 tablespoon honey
- 4 (5- to 6-ounce each) catfish fillets

1. Start by preheating the toaster oven to 425°F.
2. Combine breadcrumbs, pecans, 2 teaspoons thyme, 1 tablespoon oil, salt, pepper and 2 tablespoons water.
3. In another bowl put your asparagus, the rest of the thyme, honey, salt, and pepper and toss.
4. Spread the asparagus in a flat layer on a baking sheet. Sprinkle a quarter of the breading over the asparagus.
5. Lay the catfish over the asparagus and press the rest of the breadcrumb mixture into each piece. Roast for 12 minutes.

Nutrition
Calories: 531, Sodium: 291 mg, Dietary Fiber: 6.1 g, Total Fat: 30.4 g, Total Carbs: 31.9 g, Protein: 34.8 g.

Parmesan-Crusted Pork Loin

In my opinion, pork loin is great no matter how you cook it, but the baked-on, parmesan-crusted style is the kind of enjoyable meal that the family will be talking about all week.

Servings: 4
Prep Time: 10 Minutes
Cook Time: 20 Minutes

1 pound pork loin
1 teaspoon salt
1/2 tablespoon garlic powder
1/2 tablespoon onion powder
2 tablespoons parmesan cheese
1 tablespoon olive oil

1. Start by preheating your toaster oven to 475°F.
2. Place the pan in the oven and let it heat while the oven preheats.
3. Mix all of the ingredients into a shallow dish and roll the pork loin until it is fully coated.
4. Remove the pan and sear the pork in the pan on each side.
5. Once seared, bake the pork in the pan for 20 minutes.

Nutrition

Calories: 334, Sodium: 718 mg, Dietary Fiber: 0 g, Total Fat: 20.8 g, Total Carbs: 1.7 g, Protein: 33.5 g.

Persimmon Toast
with Sour Cream & Cinnamon

You don't find many persimmon recipes, but this one may have you looking for more. It has the perfect taste and texture for a light midmorning or early-evening snack.

Servings: 1
Prep Time: 5 Minutes
Cook Time: 5 Minutes

1 slice of wheat bread
1/2 persimmon
Sour cream to taste
Sugar to taste
Cinnamon to taste

1. Spread a thin layer of sour cream across the bread.
2. Slice the persimmon into 1/4 inch pieces and lay them across the bread.
3. Sprinkle cinnamon and sugar over the persimmon.
4. Toast with your toaster oven until the bread and persimmon begins to brown.

Nutrition
Calories: 89, Sodium: 133 mg, Dietary Fiber: 2.0 g, Total Fat: 1.1 g, Total Carbs: 16.5 g, Protein: 3.8 g.

Roasted Beet Salad
with Oranges & Beet Greens

This is a sweet treat for someone who is looking for a substantial snack with a little flavor.

Servings: 6
Prep Time: 1 1/2 hours
Cook Time: 1 1/2 hours

6 medium beets with beet greens attached
2 large oranges
1 small sweet onion, cut into wedges
1/3 cup red wine vinegar
1/4 cup extra-virgin olive oil
2 garlic cloves, minced
1/2 teaspoon grated orange peel

1. Start by preheating the toaster oven to 400°F.
2. Trim leaves from beets and chop, then set aside.
3. Pierce beets with a fork and place in a roasting pan.
4. Roast beets for 1-1/2 hours.
5. Allow beets to cool, peel, then cut into 8 wedges and put into a bowl.
6. Place beet greens in a sauce pan and cover with just enough water to cover. Heat until water boils, then immediately remove from heat.
7. Drain greens and press to remove liquid from greens, then add to beet bowl.
8. Remove peel and pith from orange and segment, adding each segment to the bowl.
9. Add onion to beet mixture. In a separate bowl mix together vinegar, oil, garlic and orange peel.
10. Combine both bowls and toss, sprinkle with salt and pepper.
11. Let stand for an hour before serving.

Nutrition
Calories: 214, Sodium: 183 mg, Dietary Fiber: 6.5 g, Total Fat: 8.9 g, Total Carbs: 32.4 g, Protein: 4.7 g.

Roasted Grape
and Goat Cheese Crostinis

I love trying new and weird recipes. Most of them don't make the cut, but this one has become one of my favorite new dishes.

Servings: 10
Prep Time: 30 Minutes
Cook Time: 5 Minutes

1 pound seedless red grapes
1 teaspoon chopped rosemary
4 tablespoons olive oil
1 rustic French baguette
1 cup sliced shallots
2 tablespoons unsalted butter
8 ounces goat cheese
1 tablespoon honey

1. Start by preheating the toaster oven to 400°F.
2. Toss grapes, rosemary, and 1 tablespoon of olive oil in a large bowl.
3. Transfer to a roasting pan and roast for 20 minutes.
4. Remove the pan from the oven and set aside to cool.
5. Slice the baguette into 1/2-inch-thick pieces..
6. Brush each slice with olive oil and place on baking sheet.
7. Bake for 8 minutes, then remove from oven and set aside.
8. In a medium skillet add butter and one tablespoon of olive oil.
9. Add shallots and sauté for about 10 minutes.
10. Mix goat cheese and honey in a medium bowl, then pour in entire shallot pan and mix thoroughly.
11. Spread shallot mixture onto baguette, top with grapes, and serve.

Nutrition
Calories: 238, Sodium: 139 mg, Dietary Fiber: 0.6 g, Total Fat: 16.3 g, Total Carbs: 16.4 g, Protein: 8.4 g.

Roasted Delicata Squash with Kale

The idea that the toaster oven is a substandard cooking device goes right out the kitchen window when you can cook a high-class meal like this one.

Servings: 2
Prep Time: 5 Minutes
Cook Time: 10 Minutes

1 medium delicata squash
1 bunch kale
1 clove garlic
2 tablespoons olive oil
Salt and pepper

1. Start by preheating your toaster oven to 425°F.
2. Clean the squash and cut off each end. Cut the squash in half and remove the seeds. Quarter the halves.
3. Toss the squash in 1 tablespoon of olive oil.
4. Place the squash on a greased baking sheet and roast for 25 minutes, turning halfway through.
5. Rinse kale and remove stems. Chop garlic.
6. Heat the leftover oil in a medium skillet and add kale and salt to taste.
7. Sauté the kale until it darkens, then mix in the garlic.
8. Cook for another minute then remove from heat and add 2 tablespoons of water.
9. Remove squash from oven and lay it on top of the garlic kale.
10. Top with salt and pepper to taste and serve.

Nutrition
Calories: 159, Sodium: 28 mg, Dietary Fiber: 1.8 g, Total Fat: 14.2 g, Total Carbs: 8.2 g, Protein: 2.6 g.

Skinny Black Bean Flautas

Flautas are excellent for a low calorie snack or a stand-out appetizer for a party. They are quick to make and not ingredient-heavy, so you don't need to put a lot of grocery planning into this dish.

Servings: 10
Prep Time: 10 Minutes
Cook Time: 25 Minutes

- 2 (15-ounce) cans black beans
- 1 cup shredded cheddar
- 1 (4-ounce) can diced green chilies
- 2 teaspoons taco seasoning
- 10 (8-inch) whole wheat flour tortillas
- Olive oil

1. Start by preheating your toaster oven to 350°F.
2. Drain the black beans, put them in a medium bowl and mash them with a fork.
3. Mix in cheese, chilies, and taco seasoning until all ingredients are even throughout.
4. Evenly spread the mixture over each tortilla and wrap tightly.
5. Brush each side lightly with olive oil and place on a baking sheet.
6. Bake for 12 minutes, turn, and bake for another 13 minutes.

Nutrition

Calories: 367, Sodium: 136 mg, Dietary Fiber: 14.4 g, Total Fat: 2.8 g, Total Carbs: 64.8 g, Protein: 22.6 g.

Turkey-Stuffed Peppers

Just the name of this meal makes your mouth start to water, and wait until the smell starts to fill your kitchen. There are so many flavors combined in this recipe and they complement each other perfectly.

Servings: 6
Prep Time: 20 Minutes
Cook Time: 35 Minutes

1 pound lean ground turkey meat
1 tablespoon olive oil
2 cloves garlic, minced
1/3 onion, minced
1 tablespoon cilantro (optional)
1 teaspoon garlic powder
1 teaspoon cumin powder
1/2 teaspoon salt
Pepper to taste
3 large red bell peppers
1 cup chicken broth
1/4 cup tomato sauce
1 1/2 cups cooked brown rice
1/4 cup shredded cheddar
6 green onions

1. Start by preheating your toaster oven to 400°F.
2. Heat a skillet on medium heat.
3. Add olive oil to the skillet, then mix in onion and garlic.
4. Sauté for about 5 minutes or until the onion starts to look opaque.
5. Add the turkey to the skillet and season with cumin, garlic powder, salt, and pepper.
6. Brown the meat until thoroughly cooked, then mix in chicken broth and tomato sauce.
7. Reduce heat and simmer for about 5 minutes, stirring occasionally.
8. Add the brown rice and continue stirring until it is evenly spread through the mix.
9. Cut the bell peppers lengthwise down the middle and remove all of the seeds.
10. Grease a pan or line it with parchment paper and lay all peppers in the pan with the outside facing down.
11. Spoon the meat mixture evenly into each pepper and use the back of the spoon to level it out.
12. Bake for 30 minutes.
13. Pull the pan out and sprinkle cheddar over each pepper, then put it back in for another 3 minutes or until the cheese is melted.
14. While the cheese melts, dice your green onions. Remove the pan from the oven and sprinkle the diced green onions over each pepper and serve.

Nutrition

Calories: 394, Sodium: 493 mg, Dietary Fiber: 4.1 g, Total Fat: 12.9 g, Total Carbs: 44.4 g, Protein: 27.7 g.

Spice-Roasted Almonds

Nuts are a great healthy snack, and they have a lot of flavor by themselves. Unfortunately, nuts can get a little bland if you over roast them. This recipe breathes new life into an old standard.

Servings: 32
Prep Time: 5 Minutes
Cook Time: 10 Minutes

1 tablespoon chili powder
1 tablespoon olive oil
1/2 teaspoon salt
1/2 teaspoon ground cumin
1/2 teaspoon ground coriander
1/4 teaspoon ground cinnamon
1/4 teaspoon black pepper
2 cups whole almonds

1. Start by preheating the toaster oven to 350°F.
2. Mix olive oil, chili powder, coriander, cinnamon, cumin, salt, and pepper.
3. Add in almonds and toss together.
4. Transfer to a baking pan and bake for 10 minutes.

Nutrition

Calories: 39, Sodium: 37 mg, Dietary Fiber: 0.8 g, Total Fat: 3.5 g, Total Carbs: 1.4 g, Protein: 1.3 g.

Spiralized Parsnip
and Sweet Potato Latkes

Parsnips have so many health benefits, but the problem is that not many people know what to do with them. When you combine them with sweet potatoes, you create a healthy snack that makes everyone happy.

Servings: 12
Prep Time: 20 Minutes
Cook Time: 20 Minutes

1 medium sweet potato
1 large parsnip
4 cups water
1 egg + 1 egg white
2 scallions
1/2 teaspoon garlic powder
1/2 teaspoon sea salt
1/2 teaspoon ground pepper

1. Start by spiralizing the sweet potato and parsnip and chopping the scallions, only reserving the green parts.
2. Preheat the toaster oven to 425°F.
3. Bring 4 cups of water to a boil. Place all of your noodles in a colander and pour the boiling water over the top, draining well.
4. Let the noodles cool, then grab handfuls and place them in a paper towel, squeeze them to remove as much liquid as possible.
5. In a large bowl, beat egg and egg white together. Add noodles, scallions, garlic powder, salt, and pepper, mix well.
6. Prepare a baking sheet and scoop out 1/4 cup of mix at a time and place it on the baking sheet.
7. Press each scoop down slightly with your hands then bake for 20 minutes, flipping half way through.

Nutrition
Calories: 24, Sodium: 91 mg, Dietary Fiber: 1.0 g, Total Fat: 0.4 g, Total Carbs: 4.3 g, Protein: 0.9 g.

Sweet Potato Chips

This is a healthy alternative to potato chips, and to be honest, these chips bring a lot more flavor to the table.

Servings: 2
Prep Time: 5 Minutes
Cook Time: 40 Minutes

2 sweet potatoes
Salt and pepper to taste
Olive oil
Cinnamon

1. Start by preheating your toaster oven to 400°F.
2. Cut off each end of the potato and discard.
3. Cut the potatoes into 1/2-inch slices.
4. Brush a pan with olive oil and lay potatoe slices flat on the pan.
5. Bake for 20 minutes, then flip and bake for another 20.

Nutrition
Calories: 139, Sodium: 29 mg, Dietary Fiber: 8.2 g, Total Fat: 0.5 g, Total Carbs: 34.1 g, Protein: 1.9 g.

Country Comfort
Corn Bread

Few foods say country comfort like a good corn bread. This is a simple recipe that brings that country comfort into your home.

Servings: 12
Prep Time: 10 Minutes
Cook Time: 20 Minutes

1 cup yellow cornmeal
1 1/2 cups oatmeal
1/4 teaspoon salt
1/4 cup granulated sugar
2 teaspoons baking powder
1 cup milk
1 large egg
1/2 cup applesauce

1. Start by blending the oatmeal into a fine powder.
2. Preheat the toaster oven to 400°F.
3. Mix oatmeal, cornmeal, salt, sugar, and baking powder, stir to blend.
4. Add milk, egg, and applesauce, and mix well.
5. Pour into a pan and bake for 20 minutes.

Nutrition
Calories: 113, Sodium: 71 mg, Dietary Fiber: 1.9 g, Total Fat: 1.9 g, Total Carbs: 21.5 g, Protein: 3.4 g.

Perfect Size French Fries

Homemade fries always beat those freezer bag ones. This recipe is awesome not only because they taste great, but because the portion size is perfect.

Servings: 1
Prep Time: 10 Minutes
Cook Time: 30 Minutes

1 medium potato
1 tablespoon olive oil
Salt and pepper to taste

1. Start by preheating your oven to 425°F.
2. Clean the potato and cut it into fries or wedges.
3. Place fries in a bowl of cold water.
4. Dry the fries on a thick sheet of paper towels and pat the tops dry.
5. Toss in a bowl with oil, salt, and pepper.
6. Bake for 30 minutes

Nutrition

Calories: 284, Sodium: 13 mg, Dietary Fiber: 4.7 g, Total Fat: 14.2 g, Total Carbs: 37.3 g, Protein: 4.3 g.

Portobello Pesto Burgers

This is an excellent vegetarian—not vegan—meal that is easy to prepare and proves that going vegetarian doesn't mean leaving the flavor behind.

Servings: 4
Prep Time: 10 Minutes
Cook Time: 26 Minutes

4 portobello mushrooms
1/4 cup sundried tomato pesto
4 whole-grain hamburger buns
1 large ripe tomato
1 log fresh goat cheese
8 large fresh basil leaves

1. Start by preheating your toaster oven to 425°F.
2. Place the mushrooms on a pan, round sides facing up.
3. Bake for 14 minutes.
4. Pull out tray, flip the mushrooms and spread 1 tablespoon of pesto on each piece.
5. Return to oven and bake for another 10 minutes.
6. Remove the mushrooms and toast the buns for 2 minutes.
7. Remove the buns and build the burger by placing tomatoes, mushroom, 2 slices of cheese, and a sprinkle of basil, then topping with the top bun.

Nutrition

Calories: 297, Sodium: 346 mg, Dietary Fiber: 1.8 g, Total Fat: 18.1 g, Total Carbs: 19.7 g, Protein: 14.4 g.

Parmigiano Reggiano
and Prosciutto Toasts with Balsamic Glaze

This entrée may be hard to say, but it sure does taste great. People will never believe that you cooked this meal in a toaster oven.

Servings: 8
Prep Time: 25 Minutes
Cook Time: 15 Minutes

- 3 ounces thinly sliced prosciutto, cut crosswise into 1/4-inch-wide strips
- 1 (3-ounce) piece Parmigiano Reggiano cheese
- 1/2 cup balsamic vinegar
- 1 medium red onion, thinly sliced
- 1 loaf ciabatta, cut into 3/4-inch-thick slices
- 1 tablespoon extra-virgin olive oil
- 1 clove garlic
- Black pepper to taste

1. Preheat your toaster oven to 350°F.
2. Place the onion in a bowl of cold water and let sit for 10 minutes.
3. Bring your vinegar to a boil, then reduce heat and simmer for 5 minutes.
4. Remove from heat completely and set aside to allow the vinegar to thicken.
5. Drain the onion.
6. Brush the tops of each bun with oil, rub with garlic, and sprinkle with pepper.
7. Use a vegetable peeler to make large curls of Parmigiano
8. Reggiano cheese and place them on the bun.
9. Bake for 15 minutes or until the bread just starts to crisp.
10. Sprinkle prosciutto and onions on top, then drizzle vinegar and serve.

Nutrition
Calories: 154, Sodium: 432 mg, Dietary Fiber: 1.0 g, Total Fat: 5.6 g, Total Carbs: 17.3 g, Protein: 8.1 g.

Philly Cheesesteak
Egg Rolls

Who doesn't love a good cheesesteak? The only negative thing about a cheesesteak is that it can get a little messy. This is fixed by sliding the ingredients into an easily portable egg roll.

Servings: 4-5
Prep Time: 20 Minutes
Cook Time: 20 Minutes

1 egg
1 tablespoon milk
2 tablespoons olive oil
1 small red onion
1 small red bell pepper
1 small green bell pepper
1 pound thinly slice roast beef
8 ounces shredded pepper jack cheese
8 ounces shredded provolone cheese
8-10 egg roll skins
Salt and pepper

1. Start by preheating your toaster oven to 425°F.
2. Mix together egg and milk in a shallow bowl and set aside for later use.
3. Chop onions and bell peppers into small pieces.
4. Heat the oil in a medium sauce pan and add the onions and peppers.
5. Cook the onions and peppers for 2–3 minutes until they are softened.
6. Add roast beef to the pan and sauté for another 5 minutes.
7. Add salt and pepper to taste.
8. Add cheese and mix together until melted.
9. Remove from heat and drain liquid from pan.
10. Roll the egg roll skins flat.
11. Add equal parts of the mix to each egg roll and roll them up per the instructions on the package.
12. Brush each egg roll with the egg mixture.
13. Line a pan with parchment paper and lay egg rolls seam-side down with a gap between each roll.
14. Bake for 20–25 minutes, depending on your preference of egg roll crispness.

Nutrition

Calories: 769, Sodium: 1114 mg, Dietary Fiber: 2.1 g, Total Fat: 39.9 g, Total Carbs: 41.4 g, Protein: 58.4 g.

Seven-Layer Tostadas

In the mood for Mexican but don't want a boring old taco? A tostada is like a taco pizza and is a great meal for one, or party appetizer.

Servings: 6
Prep Time: 15 Minutes
Cook Time: 5 Minutes

- 1 (16-ounce) can refried pinto beans
- 1 1/2 cups guacamole
- 1 cup light sour cream
- 1/2 teaspoon taco seasoning
- 1 cup shredded Mexican cheese blend
- 1 cup chopped tomatoes
- 1/2 cup thinly sliced green onions
- 1/2 cup sliced black olives
- 6-8 whole wheat flour tortillas small enough to fit your oven
- Olive oil

1. Start by placing baking sheet into toaster oven while you preheat it to 450°F. Remove pan and drizzle with olive oil.
2. Place tortillas on pan and cook in oven until they are crisp, turn at least once, this should take about 5 minutes or less.
3. Put your refried beans in a medium bowl and mash them up to break apart any chunks, then microwave them for 2 1/2 minutes.
4. Stir your taco seasoning into the sour cream. Chop your vegetables and halve your olives.
5. Add your ingredients in this order: refried beans, guacamole, sour cream, shredded cheese, tomatoes, onions, and olives.

Nutrition

Calories: 657, Sodium: 581 mg, Dietary Fiber: 16.8 g, Total Fat: 31.7 g, Total Carbs: 71.3 g, Protein: 28.9 g.

Roasted-Fennel
Ditalini and Shrimp

Even shrimp can be made in a toaster oven, and the oven actually gives it a really nice baked texture; add a little pasta and you have a complete gourmet meal.

Servings: 4
Prep Time: 40 Minutes
Cook Time: 30 Minutes

1 pound extra-large, thawed, tail-on shrimp
1 teaspoon fennel seeds
1 teaspoon salt
1 fennel bulb, halved and sliced crosswise
4 chopped cloves garlic
2 tablespoons olive oil
1/2 teaspoon freshly ground black pepper
Grated zest of 1 lemon
1/2 pound whole-wheat ditalini

1. Start by preheating the toaster oven to 450°F.
2. Toast the seeds in a medium pan over medium heat for about 5 minutes, then toss with shrimp.
3. Add water and 1/2 teaspoon salt to the pan and bring the mixture to a boil.
4. Reduce heat and simmer for 30 minutes.
5. Combine fennel, garlic, oil, pepper, and remaining salt in a roasting pan.
6. Roast for 20 minutes, then add shrimp mixture and roast for another 5 minutes or until shrimp are cooked.
7. While the fennel is roasting cook your pasta per the directions on the package, drain, and set aside.
8. Remove the shrimp mixture and mix in pasta, roast for another 5 minutes.

Nutrition

Calories: 420, Sodium: 890 mg, Dietary Fiber: 4.2 g, Total Fat: 10.2 g, Total Carbs: 49.5 g, Protein: 33.9 g.

Spicy Avocado Cauliflower Toast

I'm not going to lie, this one takes some time and work, but the results are definitely worth the effort.

Servings: 2
Prep Time: 45 Minutes
Cook Time: 15 Minutes

- 1/2 a large head of cauliflower with leaves removed
- 3 1/4 teaspoons olive oil
- 1 small jalapeño
- 1 tablespoon chopped cilantro leaves
- 2 slices whole grain bread
- 1 medium avocado
- Salt and pepper
- 5 radishes
- 1 green onion
- 2 teaspoons hot sauce
- 1 lime

1. Start by preheating the toaster oven to 450°F.
2. Cut the cauliflower into thick pieces, about 3/4 inches, and slice the jalapeno into thin slices.
3. Place the cauliflower and jalapeno in a bowl and mix together with 2 teaspoons olive oil.
4. Add salt and pepper to taste and mix for another minute.
5. Coat a pan with another teaspoon of olive oil then lay the cauliflower mixture flat across the pan.
6. Cook for 20 minutes, flipping in the last 5 minutes.
7. Reduce heat to toast.
8. Sprinkle cilantro over the mix while it is still warm, and set aside.
9. Brush bread with remaining oil and toast until golden brown, about 5 minutes.
10. Dice onion and radish.
11. Mash avocado in a bowl, then spread on toast and sprinkle salt and pepper to taste.
12. Put cauliflower mix on toast and cover with onion and radish. Drizzle with hot sauce and serve with a lime wedge.

Nutrition

Calories: 359, Sodium: 308 mg, Dietary Fiber: 11.1 g, Total Fat: 28.3 g, Total Carbs: 26.4 g, Protein: 6.6 g.

Squash and Zucchini Mini Pizza

This recipe is the perfect combination of happy and healthy. It is packed with healthy vegetables, but doesn't taste like health food.

Servings: 4
Prep Time: 25 Minutes
Cook Time: 15 Minutes

1 pizza crust
1/2 cup parmesan cheese
4 tablespoons oregano
1 zucchini
1 yellow summer squash
Olive oil
Salt and pepper

1. Start by preheating your toaster oven to 350°F.
2. If you are using homemade crust, roll out 8 mini portions; if it is store-bought, use a cookie cutter to cut out the portions.
3. Sprinkle parmesan and oregano equally on each piece. Layer the zucchini and squash in a circle – one on top of the other – around the entire circle.
4. Brush with olive oil and sprinkle salt and pepper to taste.
5. Bake for 15 minutes and serve.

Nutrition

Calories: 151, Sodium: 327 mg, Dietary Fiber: 3.1 g, Total Fat: 8.6 g, Total Carbs: 10.3 g, Protein: 11.4 g.

Basic Roasted Tofu

Most people find tofu to be bland and boring, but I see it as a blank slate that you can dress up any way you desire. This one takes a little time, but it is well worth it in the taste department and ludicrously simple to make.

Servings: 4
Prep Time: 1 Hour
Cook Time: 45 Minutes

1 or more (16-ounce) containers extra-firm tofu
1 tablespoon sesame oil
1 tablespoon soy sauce
1 tablespoon rice vinegar
1 tablespoon water

1. Start by drying the tofu: first pat dry with paper towels, then lay on another set of paper towels or even a dish towel.
2. Put a plate on top of the tofu then put something heavy on the plate (like a large can of vegetables). Leave it there for as long as you can, at least 20 minutes.
3. While tofu is being pressed, whip up marinade by combining oil, soy sauce, vinegar, and water in a bowl and set aside.
4. Cut the tofu into squares or sticks. Place the tofu in the marinade for at least 30 minutes.
5. Preheat your toaster oven to 350°F. Line a pan with parchment paper and add as many pieces of tofu as you can while giving each piece adequate space.
6. Bake for 20–45 minutes; it is done when the outside edges look golden brown. Time will vary depending on tofu size and shape.

Nutrition
Calories: 114, Sodium: 239 mg, Dietary Fiber: 1.1 g, Total Fat: 8.1 g, Total Carbs: 2.2 g, Protein: 9.5 g.

Butter Fish
with Sake and Miso

Many people don't realize that you can use a toaster oven to cook fish; in fact, you can use it to cook some of the most delicious fish you will ever eat.

Servings: 4
Prep Time: 15 Minutes + Marinade Time
Cook Time: 11 Minutes

4 (7-ounce) pieces of butter fish
1/3 cup sake
1/3 cup mirin
2/3 cups sugar
1 cup white miso

1. Start by combining sake, mirin, and sugar in a sauce pan and bringing the ingredients to a boil.
2. Allow to boil for 5 minutes, then reduce heat and simmer for another 10 minutes.
3. Remove from heat completely and mix in miso.
4. Marinate the fish in the mixture for as long as possible, up to 3 days if possible.
5. Preheat toaster oven to 450°F and bake for 8 minutes.
6. Switch your setting to broil and broil the fish for another 2-3 minutes until the sauce is caramelized.

Nutrition
Calories: 529, Sodium: 2892 mg, Dietary Fiber: 3.7 g, Total Fat: 5.8 g, Total Carbs: 61.9 g, Protein: 53.4 g.

Chicken Breast
with Rosemary

Sometimes it is the simpler dishes that are the best, as proven by these delicious and juicy chicken breasts.

Servings: 4
Prep Time: 10 Minutes
Cook Time: 60 Minutes

4 bone-in chicken breast halves
3 tablespoons softened butter
1/2 teaspoon salt
1/4 teaspoon pepper
1 tablespoon rosemary
1 tablespoon extra-virgin olive oil

1. Start by preheating the toaster oven to 400°F.
2. Mix the butter, salt, pepper, and rosemary in a bowl.
3. Coat the breasts with the butter and place in a shallow pan.
4. Drizzle oil over the breasts and roast for 25 minutes.
5. Flip the chicken and roast for another 20 minutes.
6. Flip the chicken one more time and roast for a final 15 minutes.

Nutrition
Calories: 392, Sodium: 551 mg, Dietary Fiber: 0 g, Total Fat: 18.4 g, Total Carbs: 0.6 g, Protein: 55.4 g.

Dijon and Swiss
Croque Monsieur

It may just be a fancy ham and cheese sandwich, but it is one spectacular fancy ham and cheese sandwich.

Servings: 2
Prep Time: 5 Minutes
Cook Time: 13 Minutes

- 4 slices of white bread
- 2 tablespoons unsalted butter
- 1 tablespoon all-purpose flour
- 1/2 cup whole milk
- 3/4 cups shredded Swiss cheese
- 1/4 teaspoon freshly ground black pepper
- 1/8 teaspoon salt
- 1 tablespoon Dijon mustard
- 4 slices ham

1. Start by cutting the crusts off the bread and placing them on a pan lined with parchment paper.
2. Melt the 1 tablespoon of butter in a sauce pan then tab the top sides of each piece of bread with butter.
3. Toast the bread in your oven for 3-5 minutes until each piece is golden brown.
4. Melt the second tablespoon of butter in the sauce pan and add the flour, mix together until they form a paste.
5. Add the milk and continue to mix until the sauce begins to thicken.
6. Remove from heat and mix in 1 tablespoon of Swiss cheese, salt, and pepper; continue stirring until cheese is melted.
7. Flip the bread over in the pan so the untoasted side is facing up.
8. Set two slices aside and spread Dijon on the other two slices.
9. Add ham and sprinkle 1/4 cup Swiss over each piece.
10. Broil for about 3 minutes.
11. Top the sandwiches off with the other slices of bread, soft side down.
12. Top with sauce and sprinkle with remaining Swiss. Toast for another 5 minutes or until the cheese is golden brown.
13. Serve immediately.

Nutrition

Calories: 452, Sodium: 1273 mg, Dietary Fiber: 1.6 g, Total Fat: 30.5 g, Total Carbs: 19.8 g, Protein: 24.4 g.

Kalamata Mozarella
Pita Melts

This is the kind of recipe that seems like one day someone said "I want to do something a little different." That day a delicious lunch sandwich was born, and now you too can enjoy it.

Servings: 2
Prep Time: 10 Minutes
Cook Time: 5 Minutes

2 (6-inch) whole wheat pitas
1 teaspoon extra-virgin olive oil
1 cup grated part-skim mozzarella cheese
1/4 small red onion
1/4 cup pitted Kalamata olives
2 tablespoons chopped fresh herbs such as parsley, basil, or oregano

1. Start by preheating your toaster oven to 425°F.
2. Brush the pita on both sides with oil and warm in the oven for one minute.
3. Dice onions and halve olives.
4. Sprinkle mozzarella over each pita and top with onion and olive.
5. Return to the oven for another 5 minutes or until the cheese is melted.
6. Sprinkle herbs over the pita and serve.

Nutrition
Calories: 387, Sodium: 828 mg, Dietary Fiber: 7.4 g, Total Fat: 16.2 g, Total Carbs: 42.0 g, Protein: 23.0 g.

Tomato Avocado Melt

This recipe is all kinds of amazing and will surely become a family favorite in your home. It is light, quick, and delicious, on top of being relatively healthy.

Servings: 2
Prep Time: 5 Minutes
Cook Time: 4 Minutes

4 slices of bread
1-2 tablespoon mayonnaise
Cayenne pepper
1 small Roma tomato
1/2 avocado
8 slices of cheese of your choice

1. Start by slicing your avocado and tomato and set aside.
2. Spread mayonnaise on the bread.
3. Sprinkle cayenne pepper over the mayo to taste.
4. Layer tomato and avocado on top of each other.
5. Top with cheese and put on greased baking sheet.
6. Broil on high for 2–4 minutes until the cheese is melted and bread is toasted.

Nutrition

Calories: 635, Sodium: 874 mg, Dietary Fiber: 4.1 g, Total Fat: 50.1 g, Total Carbs: 17.4 g, Protein: 30.5 g.

Vegetarian Philly Sandwich

If meat isn't your thing, it doesn't mean that you should miss out on an American staple. This recipe has all of the flavor, but none of the you-know-what.

Servings: 2
Prep Time: 5 Minutes
Cook Time: 20 Minutes

2 tablespoons olive oil
8 ounces sliced portabello mushrooms
1 vidalia onion
1 green bell pepper
1 red bell pepper
Salt and pepper
4 slices 2% provolone cheese
4 rolls

1. Start by slicing your peppers and onion into thin slices.
2. Preheat the toaster oven to 475°F.
3. Heat the oil in a medium sauce over medium heat.
4. Sauté mushrooms by themselves for about 5 minutes, then add the onions and peppers and sauté for another 10 minutes.
5. Open the rolls and divide the vegetables into each roll.
6. Add the cheese and toast until the rolls start to brown and the cheese melts.

Nutrition
Calories: 645, Sodium: 916 mg, Dietary Fiber: 7.2 g, Total Fat: 33.3 g, Total Carbs: 61.8 g, Protein: 27.1 g.

CHAPTER 6

Dinner Recipes

Baked Veggie Egg Rolls

Who doesn't love a good egg roll? Not only do these egg rolls taste great, but they are a great vegetarian option.

Servings: 2
Prep Time: 10 Minutes
Cook Time: 20 Minutes

1/2 tablespoon olive or vegetable oil
2 cups thinly-sliced chard
1/4 cup grated carrot
1/2 cup chopped pea pods
3 shiitake mushrooms
2 scallions
2 medium cloves garlic
1/2 tablespoon fresh ginger
1/2 tablespoon soy sauce
6 egg roll wrappers
Olive oil spray for cookie sheet and egg rolls

1. Start by mincing mushrooms, garlic, and ginger and slicing scallions.
2. Heat oil on medium heat in a medium skillet and char peas, carrots, scallions, and mushrooms.
3. Cook for 3 minutes, then add ginger. Stir in soy sauce and remove from heat.
4. Preheat the toaster oven to 400°F and spray the cookie sheet. Spoon even portions of vegetable mix over each egg roll and wrap them up.
5. Place egg rolls on cookie sheet and spray with olive oil. Bake for 20 minutes until egg roll shells are browned.

Nutrition
Calories: 421, Sodium: 1166 mg, Dietary Fiber: 8.2 g, Total Fat: 7.7 g, Total Carbs: 76.9 g, Protein: 13.7 g.

Broccoli and Avocado
Tacos

It is rare to find the words "delicious," "vegan," and "gluten free" in the same sentence, but here they are. This is an amazing entrée that meets all of those requirements and is easy to throw together in a short period of time.

Servings: 3
Prep Time: 25 Minutes
Cook Time: 5 Minutes

6-10 authentic Mexican corn tortillas
1 large ripe avocado
1 large head broccoli
6-8 white mushrooms, sliced
1/2 bunch cilantro
1/2 teaspoon garlic powder
Sea salt and pepper
Olive oil

1. Start by preheating your toaster oven to 400°F.
2. Slice avocado into thin slices and chop the broccoli into bite-sized florets.
3. Arrange the broccoli and mushrooms on a baking sheet and drizzle oil and sprinkle salt, pepper, and garlic powder over the veggies.
4. Bake them for 20 minutes. Warm the tortillas then fill with mushrooms and broccoli, and top with avocado.
5. Sprinkle cilantro over the tacos and serve.

Nutrition

Calories: 313, Sodium: 99 mg, Dietary Fiber: 12.6 g, Total Fat: 15.3 g, Total Carbs: 40.5 g, Protein: 10.4 g.

Broiled Tilapia
with Parmesan and Herbs

Tilapia is a great fish to cook because its mild flavor goes well with many recipes like this one: the tilapia is the main ingredient but the parmesan and herbs take center stage.

Servings: 4
Prep Time: 25 Minutes
Cook Time: 8 Minutes

- 4 (6- to 8-ounce) farm-raised tilapia fillets
- 1/2 cup freshly grated parmesan cheese
- 2 tablespoons low-fat mayonnaise
- 2 tablespoons light sour cream
- 2 tablespoons melted unsalted butter
- 2 tablespoons lemon juice
- 1/2 teaspoon dried basil
- 1/2 teaspoon dried tarragon
- 1/8 teaspoon onion powder
- Salt and pepper to taste

1. Mix together 1/4 cup parmesan and all other ingredients, except tilapia.
2. Place the mixture in a plastic zipper bag, add fish and toss.
3. Place fish mixture in a shallow pan and set aside to marinate for 20 minutes.
4. Place the fish in a broiler pan and top with a few spoonful of marinade and sprinkle the rest of the parmesan over the fish.
5. Broil until lightly browned, around 8 minutes.

Nutrition
Calories: 369, Sodium: 459 mg, Dietary Fiber: 0 g, Total Fat: 17.7 g, Total Carbs: 2.0 g, Protein: 51.6 g.

Coconut-Crusted Haddock
with Curried Pumpkin Seeds

One of the hardest parts of eating healthy is to find foods that don't taste like "health foods." This recipe does a great job at keeping the calories low, but letting the flavor fly.

Serve: 4
Prep Time: 20 Minutes
Cook Time: 10 Minutes

- 2 teaspoons canola oil
- 2 teaspoons honey
- 1 teaspoon curry powder
- 1/4 teaspoon ground cinnamon
- 1 teaspoon salt
- 1 cup pumpkin seeds
- 1 1/2 pounds haddock or cod filets
- 1/2 cup roughly grated unsweetened coconut
- 3/4 cups panko-style bread crumbs
- 2 tablespoons butter, melted
- 3 tablespoons apricot fruit spread
- 1 tablespoon lime juice

1. Start by preheating the toaster oven to 350°F.
2. In a medium bowl, mix honey, oil, curry powder, 1/2 teaspoon salt, and cinnamon.
3. Add pumpkin seeds to the bowl and toss to coat, then lay them flat on a baking sheet.
4. Toast for 14 minutes, then transfer to a bowl to cool.
5. Increase the oven temperature to 450°F.
6. Brush a baking sheet with oil and lay filets flat.
7. In another medium mixing bowl, mix together bread crumbs, butter, and remaining salt.
8. In a small bowl mash together apricot spread and lime juice.
9. Brush each filet with apricot mixture, then press bread crumb mixture onto each piece.
10. Bake for 10 minutes.
11. Transfer to a plate and top with pumpkin seeds to serve.

Nutrition

Calories: 273, Sodium: 491 mg, Dietary Fiber: 6.1 g, Total Fat: 8.4 g, Total Carbs: 47.3 g, Protein: 7.0 g.

Tex-Mex Chicken Quesadillas

Quesadillas are like pizza, everyone loves them and there is no such thing as a bad one. This recipe is simple, but still filled with Tex-Mex flavor.

Servings: 4
Prep Time: 10 Minutes
Cook Time: 10 Minutes

2 green onions
2 cups shredded skinless rotisserie chicken meat
1 1/2 cups shredded Monterey Jack cheese
1 pickled jalapeño
1/4 cup fresh cilantro leaves
4 burrito-size flour tortillas
1/2 cup reduced-fat sour cream

1. Start by preheating the toaster oven to 425°F.
2. Thinly slice the green onions and break apart.
3. Mix together chicken, cheese, jalapeno, and onions in a bowl, then evenly divide the mixture onto one half of each tortilla.
4. Fold each half over the mixture and place each quesadilla onto a baking sheet.
5. Bake for 10 minutes.
6. Cut in half or quarters and serve with sour cream.

Nutrition

Calories: 830, Sodium: 921 mg, Dietary Fiber: 1.8 g, Total Fat: 59.0 g, Total Carbs: 13.8 g, Protein: 60.8 g.

Oven-Fried Herbed Chicken

This recipe screams comfort food and offers that crunch that we love with our chicken. The best part is that there is nothing complicated about it, there are just a few steps between you and perfect flavor.

Servings: 2
Prep Time: 10 Minutes + Marinate Time
Cook Time: 15 Minutes

1/2 cup buttermilk
2 cloves garlic, minced
1 1/2 teaspoons salt
1 tablespoon oil
1/2 pound boneless, skinless chicken breasts
1 cup rolled oats
1/2 teaspoon red pepper flakes
1/2 cup grated parmesan cheese
1/4 cup fresh basil leaves or rosemary needles
Olive oil spray

1. Mix together buttermilk, oil, 1/2 teaspoon salt, and garlic in a shallow bowl.
2. Roll the chicken in the buttermilk and leave in the bowl, refrigerate overnight.
3. Preheat your toaster oven to 425°F.
4. Mix together the oats, red pepper, salt, parmesan, and basil, and mix roughly to break up oats.
5. Place the mixture on a plate.
6. Remove the chicken from the buttermilk mixture and let any excess drip off.
7. Roll the chicken in the oat mixture and transfer to a baking sheet lightly coated with olive oil spray.
8. Spray the chicken with oil spray and bake for 15 minutes.

Nutrition

Calories: 651, Sodium: 713 mg, Dietary Fiber: 4.4 g, Total Fat: 31.2 g, Total Carbs: 34.1 g, Protein: 59.5 g.

Miso-Glazed Salmon

This is another case of cooking gourmet fish in a toaster oven. It may seem questionable, but the results are always worth the trial.

Servings: 4
Prep Time: 10 Minutes
Cook Time: 5 Minutes

1/4 cup red or white miso
1/3 cup sake
1 tablespoon soy sauce
2 tablespoons vegetable oil
1/4 cup sugar
4 skinless salmon filets

1. In a shallow bowl, mix together the miso, sake, oil, soy sauce, and sugar.
2. Toss the salmon in the mixture until thoroughly coated on all sides.
3. Preheat your toaster oven to "high," on broil mode.
4. Place the salmon in a broiling pan and broil until the top is well charred—about 5 minutes.

Nutrition

Calories: 401, Sodium: 315 mg, Dietary Fiber: 0 g, Total Fat: 19.2 g, Total Carbs: 14.1 g, Protein: 39.2 g.

Pesto & White Wine Salmon

This is another entry in the category of fish too delicious to actually be called fish. It is simple to make and will win over even the most staunch fish hater.

Servings: 4
Prep Time: 20 Minutes
Cook Time: 10 Minutes

1 1/4 pounds salmon filet
2 tablespoons white wine
2 tablespoons pesto
1 lemon

1. Cut the salmon into 4 pieces and place on a greased baking sheet.
2. Slice the lemon into quarters and squeeze 1 quarter over each piece of salmon.
3. Drizzle wine over salmon and set aside to marinate while you preheat the toaster oven on broil.
4. Spread pesto over each piece of salmon.
5. Broil for at least 10 minutes or until the fish is cooked to your liking and the pesto is browned.

Nutrition
Calories: 236, Sodium: 111 mg, Dietary Fiber: 0.9 g, Total Fat: 12.1 g, Total Carbs: 3.3 g, Protein: 28.6 g.

Rigatoni
with Roasted Broccoli and Chick Peas

There is no shortage of pasta recipes out there, but most of them are just pasta and sauce. This vegetarian recipe lets the pasta shine without a heavy sauce.

Servings: 4
Prep Time: 30 Minutes
Cook Time: 10 Minutes

1 can anchovies packed in oil
4 cloves garlic, chopped
1 can chickpeas
1 chicken bouillon cube
1 pound broccoli, cut into small florets
1/2 pound whole-wheat rigatoni
1/2 cup grated Romano cheese

1. Start by chopping the anchovies and cutting the broccoli into small florets.
2. Set the anchovy oil aside for later use.
3. Preheat your toaster oven to 450°F.
4. In a shallow sauce pan, sauté the anchovies in their oil, with garlic, until the garlic browns.
5. Drain the chickpeas, but be sure to save the canned liquid.
6. Add the chickpea liquid and bouillon to the anchovies, stir until bouillon dissolves.
7. Pour anchovy mix into a roasting pan and add broccoli and chickpeas.
8. Roast for 20 minutes.
9. While the veggies roast, cook rigatoni per the package directions; drain the pasta, saving one cup of water.
10. Add the pasta to the anchovy mix and roast for another 10 minutes. Add reserved water, stirring in a little at a time until the pasta reaches the desired consistency.
11. Top with Romano and serve.

Nutrition

Calories: 574, Sodium: 1198 mg, Dietary Fiber: 13.7 g, Total Fat: 14.0 g, Total Carbs: 81.1 g, Protein: 31.1 g.

Mozzarella & Olive Pizza Bagels

Pizza bagels are just awesome no matter what time of day it is. This particular recipe dresses up the pizza bagel to give it a little adult flair.

Servings: 4
Prep Time: 5 Minutes
Cook Time: 10 Minutes

2 whole wheat bagels
1/4 cup marinara sauce
1/4 teaspoon Italian seasoning
1/8 teaspoon red pepper flakes
3/4 cup shredded low-moisture mozzarella cheese
1/4 cup chopped green pepper
3 tablespoons sliced black olives
Fresh basil
1 teaspoon parmesan cheese

1. Start by preheating your toaster oven to 375°F and line a pan with parchment paper.
2. Cut the bagels in half and lay on the pan with inside facing up. Spread sauce over each half.
3. Sprinkle red pepper over each half. Sprinkle 2 tablespoons of mozzarella over each half.
4. Top each half with olives and peppers, then top with another tablespoon of mozzarella.
5. Bake for 8 minutes, then switch to broil setting and broil for another 2 minutes. Top with basil and parmesan and serve.

Nutrition
Calories: 222, Sodium: 493 mg, Dietary Fiber: 1.9 g, Total Fat: 6.1 g, Total Carbs: 30.2 g, Protein: 12.1 g.

Roasted Butternut Squash
with Brussels Sprouts & Sweet Potato Noodles

This is another one of those recipes that proves that vegan doesn't mean tasteless. This flavorful dish takes a bit of prep work, but is well worth it and a healthy alternative for the entire family.

Servings: 2
Prep Time: 2 Hrs 30 Minutes
Cook Time: 15 Minutes

Squash:
- 3 cups chopped butternut squash
- 2 teaspoons extra light olive oil
- 1/8 teaspoon sea salt

Veggies:
- 5-6 Brussels sprouts
- 5 fresh shiitake mushrooms
- 2 cloves garlic
- 1/2 teaspoon black sesame seeds
- 1/2 teaspoon white sesame seeds
- A few sprinkles ground pepper
- A small pinch red pepper flakes
- 1 tablespoon extra light olive oil
- 1 teaspoon sesame oil
- 1 teaspoon onion powder
- 1 teaspoon garlic powder
- 1/4 teaspoon sea salt

Noodles:
- 1 bundle sweet potato vermicelli
- 2-3 teaspoons low-sodium soy sauce

1. Start by soaking your potato vermicelli in water for at least 2 hours.
2. Preheat your toaster oven to 375°F.
3. Place squash on a baking sheet with edges, drizzle with olive oil and sprinkle with salt and pepper. Mix together well on pan.
4. Bake the squash for 30 minutes, mixing and flipping half way through.
5. Remove the stems from the mushrooms and chop the Brussels sprouts.
6. Chop garlic and mix the veggies.
7. Drizzle sesame and olive oil over the mixture, then add garlic powder, onion powder, sesame seeds, red pepper flakes, salt, and pepper.
8. Bake this veggie mix for 15 minutes.
9. While the veggies bake, put your noodles in a small sauce pan and add just enough water to cover them.
10. Bring the water to a rolling boil and boil noodles for about 8 minutes.
11. Drain the noodles and combine with the squash and veggies in a large bowl.
12. Drizzle with soy sauce, sprinkle with sesame seeds, and serve.

Nutrition
Calories: 409, Sodium: 1124 mg, Dietary Fiber: 12.2 g, Total Fat: 15.6 g, Total Carbs: 69.3 g, Protein: 8.8 g.

Spicy Sesame-Honey Chicken

This recipe is a great way to add a little flair to dinner with a bit of sugar, spice, and everything nice.

Servings: 4
Prep Time: 40 Minutes + Marinate Time
Cook Time: 30 Minutes

- 1 package of chicken thighs/wings
- 1 tablespoon sugar
- 1 1/3 tablespoons chili garlic sauce
- 1/4 cup soy sauce
- 1 tablespoon sesame oil
- 1 tablespoon ketchup
- 1 tablespoon honey
- 1 tablespoon soy sauce
- 1 teaspoon sugar or brown sugar
- 1 teaspoon cornstarch

1. Create a marinade by combining 1 tablespoon chili sauce, soy sauce, and sesame oil.
2. Toss the chicken in the marinade and refrigerate for at least 30 minutes, but up to a day.
3. Preheat the toaster oven to 375°F. Place the chicken on a baking sheet with a little space between each piece and bake for 30 minutes.
4. While the chicken bakes, create the sauce by combining all the leftover ingredients including the 1/3 tablespoon of chili sauce.
5. Mix well and microwave in 30-second intervals until the sauce starts to thicken.
6. Toss the chicken in the sauce and serve.

Nutrition

Calories: 401, Sodium: 1439 mg, Dietary Fiber: 0 g, Total Fat: 16.0 g, Total Carbs: 11.2 g, Protein: 50.6 g.

Fennel & Tomato Chicken Paillard

This style of cooking is not as popular as it once was, but this is an awesome way to cook a tasty meal for one in just a few minutes.

Servings: 1
Prep Time: 5 Minutes
Cook Time: 12 Minutes

1/4 cup olive oil
1 boneless skinless chicken breast
Salt and pepper
1 garlic clove, thinly sliced
1 small diced Roma tomato
1/2 fennel bulb, shaved
1/4 cup sliced mushrooms
2 tablespoons sliced black olives
1 1/2 teaspoons capers
2 sprigs fresh thyme
1 tablespoon chopped fresh parsley

1. Start by pounding the chicken until it is about 1/2-inch thick.
2. Preheat the toaster oven to 400°F and brush the bottom of a baking pan with olive oil.
3. Sprinkle salt and pepper on both sides of the chicken and place it in the baking pan.
4. In a bowl, mix together all the other ingredients including the rest of the olive oil.
5. Spoon the mix over the chicken and bake for 12 minutes.

Nutrition

Calories: 797, Sodium: 471 mg, Dietary Fiber: 6.0 g, Total Fat: 63.7 g, Total Carbs: 16.4 g, Protein: 45.8 g.

Traditional English Fish and Chips

People all around the world love themselves some fish and chips, something that is so bland, yet one of the more exotic foods in the English stable. This recipe is not bland, but it does stay true to the English tradition.

Servings: 4
Prep Time: 40 Minutes
Cook Time: 17 Minutes

1 3/4 pounds potatoes
4 tablespoons olive oil
1 1/4 teaspoons kosher salt
1 1/4 teaspoons black pepper
8 sprigs fresh thyme
4 (6-ounce) pieces cod
1 lemon
1 clove garlic
2 tablespoons capers

1. Start by preheating your toaster oven to 450°F.
2. Cut the potatoes into 1-inch chunks.
3. Combine potatoes, 2 tablespoons oil, salt, and thyme in a baking tray and toss.
4. Spread into a flat layer and bake for 30 minutes.
5. Wrap the mixture in foil to keep warm.
6. Wipe the tray with a paper towel and then lay the cod in the tray.
7. Slice the lemon and top the cod with lemon, salt, pepper, and thyme.
8. Drizzle the rest of the oil over the cod and bake for 12 minutes.
9. Place the cod and potatoes on separate pans and bake together for an additional 5 minutes.
10. Combine and serve.

Nutrition

Calories: 442, Sodium: 1002 mg, Dietary Fiber: 5.4 g, Total Fat: 15.8 g, Total Carbs: 32.7 g, Protein: 42.5 g.

Cheddar & Dijon
Tuna Melt

No matter what time of day it is, nothing beats a classic tuna melt. This recipe has just enough to make the ordinary extraordinary, without having to put in too much work.

Servings: 1
Prep Time: 5 Minutes
Cook Time: 7 Minutes

1 (6-ounce) can tuna, drained and flaked
2 tablespoons mayonnaise
1 pinch salt
1 teaspoon balsamic vinegar
1 teaspoon Dijon mustard
2 slices whole wheat bread
2 teaspoons chopped dill pickle
1/4 cup shredded sharp cheddar cheese

1. Start by preheating your toaster oven to 375°F.
2. Put your bread in in the toaster while it warms.
3. Mix together tuna, mayo, salt, vinegar, mustard, and pickle in a small bowl.
4. Remove the bread from the oven and put the tuna mix on one side and the cheese on the other.
5. Return to toaster oven and bake for 7 minutes.
6. Combine slices, cut, and serve.

Nutrition
Calories: 688, Sodium: 1024 mg, Dietary Fiber: 4.1 g, Total Fat: 35.0 g, Total Carbs: 31.0 g, Protein: 59.9 g.

Adobo Turkey Chimichangas

Chimichangas are a highly underrated Mexican food that keeps my family happy weekly. When you make them with turkey it makes them a healthier option for the family.

Servings: 4
Prep Time: 10 Minutes
Cook Time: 15 Minutes

- 1 pound thickly sliced smoked turkey from deli counter, chopped
- 1 tablespoon chili powder
- 2 cups shredded slaw cabbage
- 1 to 2 chipotles in adobo sauce
- 1 cup tomato sauce
- 3 chopped scallions
- Salt and pepper
- 4 (12-inch) flour tortillas
- 1 1/2 cups pepper jack cheese
- 2 tablespoons olive oil
- 1 cup sour cream
- 2 tablespoons chopped cilantro

1. Start by preheating toaster oven to 400°F.
2. In a medium bowl mix together turkey and chili powder.
3. Add cabbage, chipotles, tomato sauce, and scallions; mix well.
4. Season mix with salt and pepper and turn a few times.
5. Warm tortillas in a microwave or on a stove top.
6. Lay cheese flat in each tortilla and top with turkey mix.
7. Fold in top and bottom, then roll to close.
8. Brush the baking tray with oil, then place chimichangas on tray and brush with oil.
9. Bake for 15 minutes or until tortilla is golden brown.
10. Top with sour cream and cilantro and serve.

Nutrition

Calories: 638, Sodium: 1785 mg, Dietary Fiber: 4.2 g, Total Fat: 44.0 g, Total Carbs: 23.9 g, Protein: 38.4 g.

CHAPTER

7

Sides

Avocado, Tomato, & Grape Salad with Crunchy Potato Croutons

There is a lot that goes into this recipe so it takes some planning, but the end result is sure to be a crowd favorite.

Servings: 2
Prep Time: 1 Hr 35 Minutes
Cook Time: 10 Minutes

Potato croutons:
1 medium-small russet potato
2 cloves garlic
1 tablespoon extra light olive oil
1 tablespoon nutritional yeast
1/2 teaspoon garlic powder
1/2 teaspoon onion powder
1/2 teaspoon dried thyme
1/2 teaspoon dried rosemary
1/2 teaspoon dried oregano
1/2 teaspoon chili powder
1/4 teaspoon Himalayan sea salt
1/3 teaspoon cayenne pepper
Pinch red pepper flakes
Black pepper to taste

Salad:
1 cup grape tomatoes
Small handful dried cranberries
Small handful green grapes
2-3 sprigs cilantro
1 avocado
2 tablespoons extra-virgin olive oil
1 tablespoon nutritional yeast
1 tablespoon lemon juice
1/2 teaspoon pure maple syrup
1/4 teaspoon salt
Few sprinkles ground pepper
Small handful toasted pecans

1. Peel and cut potatoes into 1-inch cubes.
2. Place potatoes in water for an hour with a pinch of salt.
3. When the hour has passed, preheat the toaster oven to 450°F.
4. Drain the potatoes and dry them on multiple layers of paper towels, then return them to the bowl.
5. Peel and mince the garlic, then add it to the bowl.
6. Add the rest of the crouton ingredients to the bowl and stir together.
7. Lay potatoes across a greased baking sheet in a single layer and bake for 35 minutes, flipping halfway through.
8. Combine oil, yeast, syrup, lemon juice, salt and pepper together to create your salad dressing.
9. Slice the tomatoes in half and put in a bowl with cranberries and grapes.
10. Chop cilantro and add to bowl. Scoop out avocado and cut it into smaller pieces and add to bowl.
11. Drizzle in dressing and mix well. Add potatoes and mix again, top with pecans and serve.

Nutrition
Calories: 1032, Sodium: 560 mg, Dietary Fiber: 22.8 g, Total Fat: 84.9 g, Total Carbs: 64.2 g, Protein: 17.0 g.

Baked Parmesan Zucchini

Zucchini is an awesome alternative to less healthy sides; this recipe is so delicious that you may forget about those other sides altogether.

Servings: 4
Prep Time: 10 Minutes
Cook Time: 20 Minutes

4 zucchinis
1/2 cup grated parmesan
1/2 teaspoon dried thyme
1/2 teaspoon dried oregano
1/2 teaspoon dried basil
1/4 teaspoon garlic powder
Salt and pepper to taste
2 tablespoons olive oil
2 tablespoons chopped fresh parsley leaves

1. Start by preheating the toaster oven to 350°F.
2. Quarter the zucchini lengthwise.
3. Mix together parmesan, dried herbs, garlic powder, salt, and pepper.
4. Lay the zucchini flat on a greased pan and drizzle with olive oil.
5. Pour the parmesan mix over the zucchini.
6. Bake for 15 minutes then switch the setting to broil for another 3 minutes.

Nutrition

Calories: 189, Sodium: 295 mg, Dietary Fiber: 2.4 g, Total Fat: 13.7 g, Total Carbs: 8.1 g, Protein: 12.0 g.

Garlic & Parmesan
Bread Bites

I wouldn't trust someone who says they don't like garlic bread. These bites are a great side to pair with many dishes - I would suggest pizza or spaghetti.

Servings: 12
Prep Time: 10 Minutes
Cook Time: 7 Minutes

1. Start by cutting the bread in half and toasting it crust-side down for 2 minutes.
2. Mix the butter, garlic, and parsley together and spread over the bread.
3. Sprinkle parmesan over the bread and toast in your toaster oven for another 5 minutes.

2 ciabatta loaves
1 stick butter at room temperature
4-6 crushed garlic cloves
Chopped parsley
2 tablespoons finely grated parmesan

Nutrition
Calories: 191, Sodium: 382 mg, Dietary Fiber: 1.0 g, Total Fat: 9.4 g, Total Carbs: 21.7 g, Protein: 4.9 g.

Roasted Garlic
Fries

Regular old fries can get pretty boring, so it always helps to spice them up a bit. This recipe takes fries from a side for chicken nuggets to a side for a nice porterhouse.

Servings: 1
Prep Time: 10 Minutes
Cook Time: 30 Minutes

Roasted Garlic:

1 small head of garlic
2 teaspoons olive oil

Baked Fries:

2 medium potatoes
2 teaspoons olive oil
Salt
Pepper

Garlic Fries Topping:

1/4 cup minced parsley
1 teaspoon olive oil
1/8 teaspoon salt
2 cloves of roasted garlic

1. Start by preheating the toaster oven to 425°F and lining a baking sheet with parchment paper.
2. Remove the outer layer from the garlic and chop off the top.
3. Drizzle oil over the garlic filling the top.
4. Cut your potatoes into fries and toss with oil, salt, and pepper.
5. Lay potatoes in a single layer on a greased baking sheet with garlic head, and bake for 30 minutes, turning fries halfway through.
6. Remove two cloves of the garlic head, mince, and add parsley.
7. Stir the garlic mixture with olive oil and salt.
8. Drizzle over fries and serve.

Nutrition

Calories: 513, Sodium: 326 mg, Dietary Fiber: 10.9 g, Total Fat: 23.9 g, Total Carbs: 70.8 g, Protein: 8.2 g.

Roasted Brussels Sprouts

I have heard that Brussels sprouts are difficult to get kids to eat. This simple recipe goes miles to improve the taste and texture of this pungent vegetable.

Servings: 6
Prep Time: 5 Minutes
Cook Time: 30 Minutes

1 1/2 pounds Brussels sprouts, ends trimmed and yellow leaves removed
3 tablespoons olive oil
1 teaspoon salt
1/2 teaspoon black pepper

1. Start by preheating the toaster oven to 400°F.
2. Toss Brussels sprouts in a large bowl, drizzle with olive oil, sprinkle with salt and pepper, then toss.
3. Roast for 30 minutes.

Nutrition

Calories: 109, Sodium: 416 mg, Dietary Fiber: 4.3 g, Total Fat: 7.4 g, Total Carbs: 10.4 g, Protein: 3.9 g.

Green Mango Salad

Be careful with this side salad, it is so good that it might make the main dish jealous.

Servings: 6
Prep Time: 10 Minutes
Cook Time: 10 Minutes

1/3 cup chopped cashews
2 mangos
1/3 cup chopped fresh coriander
1/3 cup chopped mint
2 tablespoons lime juice
4 teaspoons sugar
4 teaspoons fish sauce
1 tablespoon olive oil
1/4 teaspoon Asian chili sauce
1/4 teaspoon hot pepper sauce
1 sweet red pepper, thinly sliced
1 cup thinly sliced red onion

1. Start by toasting the cashews in your toaster oven for 8 minutes.
2. Cut pointed ends off mangos, then skin.
3. Cut the mangos lengthwise into thin slices, then stack them on top of each other and cut again into thin strips.
4. In a large bowl, mix together mint, coriander, lime juice, fish sauce, sugar, olive oil, and chili sauce.
5. Add mangos, red pepper, and onions to the bowl and toss.
6. Transfer salad to plates and sprinkle with cashews before serving.

Nutrition

Calories: 140, Sodium: 317 mg, Dietary Fiber: 2.7 g, Total Fat: 6.2 g, Total Carbs: 20.7 g, Protein: 2.3 g.

Honey-Roasted Carrots
with Sesame Seeds

Never thought that carrots could actually be an exciting side dish? This recipe takes carrots to a gourmet level in a simple way.

Servings: 4
Prep Time: 5 Minutes
Cook Time: 10 Minutes

- 2 bags baby carrots
- 2 tablespoons olive oil
- 2 tablespoons honey
- Salt and pepper to taste
- 1 tablespoon soy sauce
- 1 tablespoon chopped fresh parsley
- 2 teaspoons sesame seeds

1. Start by preheating the toaster oven to 450°F.
2. Line a pan with parchment paper and put in the oven while it heats.
3. In a small bowl, mix together oil and 1 tablespoon honey.
4. Drizzle honey mixture over carrots.
5. Sprinkle with salt and pepper.
6. Roast carrots for 10 minutes.
7. Mix soy sauce and remaining honey together and toss o sn carrots.
8. Sprinkle parsley and sesame seeds over the carrots and serve.

Nutrition
Calories: 142, Sodium: 314 mg, Dietary Fiber: 3.5 g, Total Fat: 7.9 g, Total Carbs: 18.7 g, Protein: 1.3 g.

Lemon-Garlic Kale Salad

This is an awesome light salad to pair with a healthy protein like grilled chicken breast or low-fat steak. It may be light, but it holds its own in the flavor department.

Servings: 8
Prep Time: 10 Minutes
Cook Time: 10 Minutes

2 cups sliced almonds
1/3 cup lemon juice
1 teaspoon salt
1 1/2 cups olive oil
4 cloves crushed garlic
12 ounces kale, stems removed

1. Set your toaster oven to toast and toast almonds for about 5 minutes.
2. Combine lemon juice and salt in a small bowl then add olive oil and garlic, mix well and set aside.
3. Cut kale into thin ribbons. Place the kale in a bowl and sprinkle with almonds.
4. Remove garlic from dressing then add desired amount of dressing to kale and toss.
5. Add additional dressing if necessary, and serve.

Nutrition

Calories: 487, Sodium: 312 mg, Dietary Fiber: 3.7 g, Total Fat: 49.8 g, Total Carbs: 10.2 g, Protein: 6.5 g.

Lemon-Thyme Bruschetta

This is great for a side, appetizer, or snack. It is easy to whip together and doesn't take a whole lot of time either.

Servings: 10
Prep Time: 5 Minutes
Cook Time: 7 Minutes

1 baguette
8 ounces ricotta cheese
1 lemon
Salt
Freshly cracked black pepper
Honey
8 sprigs fresh thyme

1. Start by preheating the toaster oven to 425°F.
2. Thinly slice the baguette and zest lemon.
3. Mix ricotta and lemon zest together and season with salt and pepper.
4. Toast the baguette slices for 7 minutes or until they start to brown.
5. Spread ricotta mix over slices.
6. Drizzle with honey and top with thyme, then serve.

Nutrition

Calories: 60, Sodium: 71 mg, Dietary Fiber: 0.6 g, Total Fat: 2.0 g, Total Carbs: 7.6 g, Protein: 3.5 g.

Simple Roasted Asparagus

Asparagus is an awesome side and a sadly overlooked vegetable in many cases. This simple recipe showcases the brilliance of asparagus.

Servings: 4
Prep Time: 2 Minutes
Cook Time: 10 Minutes

1 bunch asparagus
4 tablespoons olive oil
Salt and pepper to taste

1. Start by preheating the toaster oven to 425°F.
2. Wash the asparagus and cut off the bottom inch.
3. Toss the asparagus in olive oil and lay flat on a baking sheet.
4. Sprinkle salt and pepper over asparagus.
5. Roast in the oven for 10 minutes.

Nutrition
Calories: 127, Sodium: 1 mg, Dietary Fiber: 0.7 g, Total Fat: 14.0 g, Total Carbs: 1.3 g, Protein: 0.7 g.

Roasted Beets
with Grapefruit Glaze

Beets are one of the more unique side dishes out there because of their undeniable flavor and sweetness. The sweetness is accented even more when we top the beets with a grapefruit vinaigrette.

Servings: 5
Prep Time: 50 Minutes
Cook Time: 10 Minutes

- 3 pounds beets
- 1 cup fresh-squeezed grapefruit juice (approximately 2 medium grapefruits)
- 1 tablespoon rice vinegar
- 3 scant tablespoons pure maple syrup
- 1 tablespoon corn starch

1. Start by preheating your toaster oven to 450°F. Place beets in a roasting pan and sprinkle them with water.
2. Roast beets until they are soft enough to be pierced with a fork, at least 40 minutes.
3. Remove beets and let them cool until you can handle them.
4. Peel skin off the beets and slice them into thin slices.
5. Mix together the grapefruit juice, syrup, and vinegar in a small bowl.
6. Pour corn starch into a medium sauce pan and slowly add grapefruit mixture. Stir together until there are no clumps.
7. Heat the sauce to a light boil then reduce heat and simmer for 5 minutes, stirring often.
8. Drizzle the glaze over the beets and serve.

Nutrition
Calories: 175, Sodium: 211 mg, Dietary Fiber: 6.0 g, Total Fat: 0.6 g, Total Carbs: 40.7 g, Protein: 4.9 g.

Rosemary & Thyme
Roasted Fingerling Potatoes

Potatoes are the perfect food for sides because they can be used in so many ways. These roasted potatoes are a great alternative to dull French fries or time-consuming baked potatoes.

Servings: 4
Prep Time: 5 Minutes
Cook Time: 25 minutes

1 small bag baby of fingerling potatoes
3 tablespoons olive oil
Salt and pepper to taste
2 teaspoons rosemary
2 teaspoons thyme

1. Start by preheating the toaster oven to 400°F.
2. Toss potatoes in olive oil and put them on a baking sheet.
3. Pierce each potato to prevent overexpansion.
4. Sprinkle salt, pepper, rosemary, and thyme over the potatoes.
5. Roast for 25 minutes.

Nutrition
Calories: 123, Sodium: 3 mg, Dietary Fiber: 1.2 g, Total Fat: 10.7 g, Total Carbs: 7.5 g, Protein: 0.9 g.

Roasted Curried Cauliflower

I like cauliflower, but it can be a little bland sometimes. This recipe helps the cauliflower out by dressing it up a little bit.

Servings: 4
Prep Time: 10 Minutes
Cook Time: 35 Minutes

1 1/2 tablespoons extra-virgin olive oil
1 teaspoon mustard seeds
1 teaspoon cumin seeds
3/4 teaspoon curry powder
3/4 teaspoon coarse salt
1 large head cauliflower
Olive oil cooking spray

1. Start by preheating the toaster oven to 375°F.
2. Mix together curry, mustard, cumin, and salt in a large bowl.
3. Break the cauliflower into pieces and add it to the bowl.
4. Toss the bowl until the cauliflower is completely covered in the spice mix.
5. Coat a baking sheet in olive oil spray and lay the cauliflower in a single layer over the sheet.
6. Roast for 35 minutes.

Nutrition

Calories: 105, Sodium: 64 mg, Dietary Fiber: 5.6 g, Total Fat: 5.9 g, Total Carbs: 11.9 g, Protein: 4.5 g.

Roasted Radishes
with Brown Butter, Lemon, and Radish Tops

I tend to embrace the spicier side of life, so it is no surprise that radishes are one of my favorite vegetables. This recipe takes something that is already great and makes it just a little better.

Servings: 4
Prep Time: 15 Minutes
Cook Time: 20 Minutes

2 bunches medium radishes
1 1/2 tablespoons olive oil
Coarse kosher salt
2 tablespoons (1/4 stick) unsalted butter
1 teaspoon fresh lemon juice

1. Start by preheating the toaster oven to 450°F.
2. Cut tops off radishes (about 1/2-inch) and coarsely chop them and set aside.
3. Cut radishes down the middle lengthwise and place in a large bowl.
4. Add olive oil to the bowl and toss to coat. Place the radishes flat side down and sprinkle with salt. Roast radishes for 20 minutes.
5. Towards the end of the roasting time, melt the butter in a small sauce pan until it browns and add lemon juice.
6. Transfer the radishes to a serving bowl and drizzle with butter, sprinkle with chopped radish tops and serve.

Nutrition
Calories: 96, Sodium: 42 mg, Dietary Fiber: 0 g, Total Fat: 11.0 g, Total Carbs: 0.1 g, Protein: 0.1 g.

Garlic & Olive Oil
Spring Vegetables

This is a great way to welcome Spring and add some variety to the dinner table.

Servings: 4
Prep Time: 10 Minutes
Cook Time: 20 Minutes

1. Start by preheating the toaster oven to 450°F.
2. Combines vegetables, garlic, oil, salt, and pepper in a bowl and toss.
3. Roast for 20 minutes or until the vegetables start to brown.

1 pound assorted spring vegetables (such as carrots, asparagus, radishes, spring onions, or sugar snap peas)
4 unpeeled garlic cloves
2 tablespoons olive oil
Salt and pepper to taste

Nutrition
Calories: 105, Sodium: 255 mg, Dietary Fiber: 4.4 g, Total Fat: 7.3 g, Total Carbs: 9.1 g, Protein: 1.8 g.

Garlic Herb Tomatoes

Tomatoes are actually a lot like potatoes in that they can be prepared as sides in many different ways. This is just one of the many delicious and healthy ways you can prepare tomatoes as a side.

Servings: 4
Prep Time: 5 Minutes
Cook Time 45 Minutes

10 medium-sized tomatoes
10 garlic cloves
Bread crumbs
Thyme
Sage
Oregano

1. Start by finely chopping garlic and herbs.
2. Cut tomatoes in half and place on a baking sheet lined with parchment paper.
3. Pour garlic and herb mixture over tomatoes.
4. Using your toaster oven, roast at 350°F for 30 minutes.
5. Top with bread crumbs and roast another 15 minutes.

Nutrition

Calories: 103, Sodium: 68 mg, Dietary Fiber: 5.4 g, Total Fat: 1.3 g, Total Carbs: 21.4 g, Protein: 4.4 g.

Roasted Vegetable and Kale Salad

This is an awesome light side that can be paired with so many dishes. It could also serve as an appetizer, or double the recipe and add some chicken for a main course.

Servings: 4
Prep Time: 10 Minutes
Cook Time: 40 Minutes

- 1 bunch kale, stems removed and chopped into ribbons
- 4 small or 2 large beets, peeled and cut roughly into 1-inch pieces
- 1/2 small butternut squash, peeled and cubed into 1-inch pieces
- 1 small red onion, sliced into 8 wedges
- 1 medium fennel bulb, sliced into 8 wedges
- 1 red pepper
- 3 tablespoons olive oil
- 1/2 cup coarsely chopped walnuts
- 3/4 teaspoon salt
- Pepper to taste
- 2 ounces goat cheese

1. Cut the beets and pepper into one-inch pieces.
2. Remove the stems from the kale and chop into thin pieces.
3. Cut fennel and red onion into wedges.
4. Preheat the toaster oven to 425°F.
5. Toss together all vegetables, except for kale, in a large bowl with oil, salt, and pepper.
6. Spread over a baking sheet and roast for 40 minutes turning halfway through.
7. At the 30-minute mark, remove the tray and sprinkle walnuts over and around the vegetables.
8. Toss the kale with dressing of choice and top with vegetables. Crumble goat cheese over the salad and serve.

Nutrition

Calories: 321, Sodium: 569 mg, Dietary Fiber: 5.5 g, Total Fat: 25.1 g, Total Carbs: 17.5 g, Protein: 11.1 g.

Traditional Greek
Spanakopita

This traditional Greek dish works great as a heavy side or even as an appetizer. It will stand out at your next get-together and garner you some kitchen recognition.

Servings: 6
Prep Time: 20 Minutes
Cook Time: 40 Minutes

- 3 tablespoons olive oil
- 2-1/2 pounds spinach
- 1 large onion
- 1 bunch green onions
- 2 cloves garlic
- 1/2 cup chopped fresh parsley
- 1/4 cup fresh dill
- 1/4 teaspoon ground nutmeg
- 2 eggs
- 1/2 cup ricotta cheese
- 1 cup crumbled feta cheese
- 3/4 teaspoon salt
- 1/2 teaspoon pepper
- 16 sheets of thawed phyllo dough
- 1/4 cup olive oil

1. Start by chopping all of your vegetables into fine pieces.
2. Preheat the toaster oven to 350°F.
3. Put the olive oil in a large skillet and heat it over medium heat.
4. Sauté onions and garlic until garlic starts to brown.
5. Add spinach, parsley, dill, and nutmeg and stir until spinach begins to wilt.
6. Break eggs in medium bowl and mix in ricotta, feta, salt, and pepper.
7. Add spinach mixture to egg mixture and stir until combined.
8. Lay a sheet of phyllo dough on a baking sheet (it should overlap the edges) and brush with oil, repeat this process 7 more times.
9. Spread the spinach mix over the dough and fold the overlapping edges in.
10. Brush the edges with olive oil. Add remaining dough one sheet at a time, brushing with oil as you go.
11. Tuck the overlapping edges down to seal the filling in the dough.
12. Bake for 40 minutes or until lightly browned.

Nutrition
Calories: 458, Sodium: 991 mg, Dietary Fiber: 5.8 g, Total Fat: 27.7 g, Total Carbs: 39.8 g, Protein: 16.9 g.

CHAPTER 8

Snacks

Baked Avocados
with Strawberry Salsa

This recipe just screams spring and it is a great light and healthy snack to enjoy on your back porch.

Servings: 3
Prep Time: 10 Minutes
Cook Time: 10 Minutes

3 avocados
Olive oil
1 cup strawberries
2 scallions
2 tablespoons goat cheese crumbles
2 tablespoons fresh basil
1 tablespoon balsamic vinegar

1. Start by stemming and quartering the strawberries and thinly slicing the basil and scallions.
2. Preheat the toaster oven to 400°F.
3. Cut the avocados in half lengthwise and remove the pit.
4. Lay the avocados on a baking sheet flesh side up and brush with olive oil.
5. Bake avocados for 8 minutes.
6. While the avocados bake mix together all the other ingredients in a medium bowl.
7. Add strawberry salsa to each avocado slice and return to the oven for another 3 minutes.
8. Serve warm.

Nutrition
Calories: 474, Sodium: 173 mg, Dietary Fiber: 60 g, Total Fat: 42.9 g, Total Carbs: 22.1 g, Protein: 7.3 g.

Baked Eggs
with Marinara and Parmesan

This recipe is simple, unique, and perfect for when you want to take snack time to a gourmet level.

Servings: 4
Prep Time: 10 Minutes
Cook Time: 15 Minutes

8 eggs
1 cup marinara sauce
1/4 cup whipping cream
1/4 cup parmesan cheese
Salt and pepper
Chives for garnish

1. Start by greasing 4 ramekins.
2. Preheat the toaster oven to 400°F.
3. Pour 1/4 cup of marinara into each ramekin.
4. Crack 2 eggs into each ramekin.
5. Top eggs with 1 tablespoon each of whipping cream and parmesan.
6. Sprinkle with salt and pepper and bake for 15 minutes.
7. While the eggs bake, chop chives.
8. Remove from oven, top with chives, and serve with toast.

Nutrition
Calories: 250, Sodium: 519 mg, Dietary Fiber: 1.6 g, Total Fat: 15.9 g, Total Carbs: 10.0 g, Protein: 17.1 g.

Easy & Quick
Bread Pudding

Bread pudding is a treat in my house, and this is my favorite recipe because it is relatively quick and easy.

Servings: 12
Prep Time: 10 Minutes
Cook Time: 40 Minutes

1 loaf bread
2 cups evaporated milk
1 cup condensed milk
1 cup raisins

1. Start by preheating the toaster oven to 400°F.
2. Pour evaporated milk into pan.
3. Add bread and mash together with hands.
4. Add condensed milk.
5. Add in raisins and stir.
6. Bake for 40 minutes, then allow to cool before cutting.

Nutrition
Calories: 329, Sodium: 475 mg, Dietary Fiber: 1.8 g, Total Fat: 7.4 g, Total Carbs: 57.2 g, Protein: 9.7 g.

Twice-Baked Sweet Potato with Coconut

This one is so decadent that it almost belongs under desserts. It is a great way to get the family to eat sweet potatoes.

Servings: 8
Prep Time: 30 Minutes
Cook Time: 20 Minutes

4 medium sweet potatoes
1/2 cup coconut milk
1 tablespoon maple syrup
1 teaspoon minced fresh ginger root
1 teaspoon adobo sauce
1/2 teaspoon salt
1/4 cup chopped pecans
1/4 cup flaked coconut

1. Scrub the sweet potatoes and pierce with a fork, then microwave for 10 minutes.
2. Cut each potato down the center lengthwise and scoop out the inside into a bowl, keep the shells.
3. Preheat the toaster oven to 350°F. Mash the potato with coconut milk, then stir in the adobo, salt, syrup, and ginger.
4. Spoon the mix back into the shells.
5. Place on a baking sheet and top with pecans and coconut.
6. Bake for 25 minutes.

Nutrition

Calories: 185, Sodium: 173 mg, Dietary Fiber: 3.2 g, Total Fat: 15.2 g, Total Carbs: 12.4 g, Protein: 2.4 g.

Zucchini Lasagna Toasts

Hold onto your seats, because this one is going to blow you away. This incredible dish could really be used for anytime, but it makes for a ridiculously awesome snack or appetizer.

Servings: 4
Prep Time: 15 Minutes
Cook Time: 10 Minutes

4 slices Italian bread
1 medium zucchini
1 clove garlic
1 tablespoon olive oil
4 ripe plum tomatoes
Salt and pepper to taste
1 cup ricotta cheese
1/4 cup freshly grated Romano cheese
4 ounces fresh mozzarella cheese

1. Start by preheating the toaster oven to 450°F. Toast bread for 10 minutes.
2. Combine oil, garlic, and zucchini in a microwave-safe bowl. Microwave on high for 4 minutes.
3. Add tomatoes, salt, and pepper to the bowl and microwave for another 3 minutes.
4. In a separate bowl mix together ricotta and Romano with salt and pepper.
5. Spread ricotta mixture on each bread slice, then top with tomato mixture.
6. Place mozzarella over each slice and place on a baking sheet.
7. Bake for 10 minutes.

Nutrition

Calories: 318, Sodium: 506 mg, Dietary Fiber: 2.2 g, Total Fat: 18.1 g, Total Carbs: 17.9 g, Protein: 22.9 g.

Mushroom Onion Strudel

Mushrooms and strudel are two foods that don't sound like they would ever go together. They work in a weird way here that is actually quite delectable.

Servings: 4 – 6
Prep Time: 20 Minutes
Cook Time: 15 Minutes

12 sheets phyllo
3 tablespoons olive oil
1 egg
1 pound mushrooms
1 medium onion
3 tablespoons butter
1 tablespoon dry sherry
1 tablespoon all-purpose flour
Leaves from 1 sprig of thyme
6 tablespoons freshly grated parmesan
Salt and pepper to taste

1. Start by preheating the toaster oven to 400°F.
2. Line a baking sheet with parchment paper.
3. Pour the oil into a skillet on medium heat and sauté the mushrooms and onions for about 7 minutes.
4. Pour in the sherry and cook at medium heat for another 3 minutes.
5. Mix in the flour, thyme salt, and pepper and remove from heat.
6. Melt butter.
7. Remove one phyllo sheet and brush one half of the sheet lengthwise with butter.
8. Fold the unbuttered side over the buttered side and smooth out any wrinkles or bubbles.
9. Again, brush one half of the phyllo with butter, and fold the unbuttered side over it again. You'll end up with one long column.
10. Place one spoonful of mushroom filling at the end of the column and sprinkle parmesan on top.
11. Fold one corner of the phyllo over the filling to create a triangle shape and keep folding over triangles until you reach the other end of the column (like folding a flag).
12. Beat the egg and brush it over the strudel. Repeat for as many strudels as you can safely fit in the sheet and bake for 15 minutes.

Nutrition

Calories: 312, Sodium: 376 mg, Dietary Fiber: 2.0 g, Total Fat: 19.2 g, Total Carbs: 25.9 g, Protein: 11.1 g.

Simply Delicious
Garlic Kale Chips

I love kale chips- they are a great healthy alternative to regular potato chips, and just like potato chips they come in all kinds of flavors.

Servings: 2
Prep Time: 5 Minutes
Cook Time: 10 Minutes

1. Start by preheating toaster oven to 350°F.
2. Tear kale into one-inch pieces and place in a bowl.
3. Add oil, pepper, garlic powder, and salt, and toss until kale is well coated.
4. Bake for 10 minutes.

4 cups kale
1 tablespoon olive oil
1/4 teaspoon pepper
1/4 teaspoon garlic powder
Salt to taste

Nutrition
Calories: 128, Sodium: 136 mg, Dietary Fiber: 2.1 g, Total Fat: 7.0 g, Total Carbs: 14.4 g, Protein: 4.1 g.

Nacho Avocado Toast

I'm not sure if there are words to describe this vegan recipe. If all vegan meals were this good, I would probably consider going vegan.

Servings: 2
Prep Time: 10 Minutes
Cook Time: 5 Minutes

2 slices of whole grain bread
3 tablespoons black bean & cilantro spread
3 tablespoons guacamole
1/2 cup baby spinach
1/4 small red onion
1/4 cup frozen sweet corn
1/4 cup plant-based nacho cheese sauce

1. Mince spinach and onion.
2. Put the corn in a strainer and run hot water over it for a minute to thaw.
3. Place the toast on a baking screen and spread with bean and cilantro spread.
4. Spread guacamole over the bean spread. Sprinkle spinach and onion over the top. Sprinkle corn over the top.
5. Toast for 4 minutes or until the toast reaches your desired level of crispiness.
6. While the bread toasts, warm the cheese sauce in the microwave or in a heat safe bowl on top of the oven.
7. Drizzle sauce over toast and serve.

Nutrition

Calories: 117, Sodium: 221 mg, Dietary Fiber: 3.6 g, Total Fat: 4.2 g, Total Carbs: 18.8 g, Protein: 4.2 g.

Parmesan Green Onion
Hash Brown Cups

These are great for a delicious snack or a breakfast surprise. They are easy to throw together and I guarantee your family will be begging for these.

Servings: 6
Prep Time: 10 Minutes
Cook Time: 75 Minutes

- 1 (20-ounce) bag hash browns, shredded
- 3 green onions
- 1/2 cup grated parmesan cheese
- 1 teaspoon kosher salt
- 1/2 teaspoon black pepper
- 2 tablespoons olive oil

1. Start by chopping the green onions.
2. Preheat the toaster oven to 350°F.
3. Combine potatoes, cheese, onion, salt, and pepper in a large bowl.
4. Drizzle olive oil over the potato mix and toss with a fork.
5. Grease a muffin tin and spoon mixture into tin.
6. Pack the mixture into each cup by pushing it down with the rounded side of the spoon.
7. Bake for 1 hour, 15 minutes.

Nutrition

Calories: 325, Sodium: 805 mg, Dietary Fiber: 3.3 g, Total Fat: 18.7 g, Total Carbs: 34.2 g, Protein: 6.2 g.

Wholesome Pita Chips

Pita chips are a delicious, healthier alternative to potato chips and are great paired with salsa or hummus.

Servings: 1
Prep Time: 5 Minutes
Cook Time: 8 Minutes

1. Start by preheating your toaster oven to 375°F.
2. Brush both sides of the pita with oil and sprinkle with salt.
3. Cut pita into 6 wedges.
4. Place wedges on ungreased baking sheet and bake for 8 minutes.

1 regular whole wheat pita
1 teaspoon olive oil
Salt to taste

Nutrition

Calories: 210, Sodium: 496 mg, Dietary Fiber: 4.7 g, Total Fat: 6.3 g, Total Carbs: 35.2 g, Protein: 6.3 g.

Tomato Whole Grain
Grilled Cheese Bites

This is a great snack for any time and any occasion. It is not super-healthy or incredibly unhealthy either; but it works as a tasty snack that can be taken on the go!

Servings: 1
Prep Time: 2 Minutes
Cook Time: 2 Minutes

4 slices fresh tomato
2 whole grain crackers
1 ounce cheddar cheese
Salt to taste

1. Start by preheating the broiler on high using your Oster toaster oven.
2. Place crackers on a cookie sheet.
3. Add tomato and sprinkle with salt.
4. Top with cheese and broil until cheese is fully melted.

Nutrition
Calories: 165, Sodium: 402 mg, Dietary Fiber: 0.8 g, Total Fat: 11.5 g, Total Carbs: 7.6 g, Protein: 8.2 g.

CHAPTER 9

Desserts

Oatmeal Raisin Cookies

Is there a food in this universe that is more polarizing than oatmeal raisin cookies? This recipe may win over a few of those people who think they don't like oatmeal raisin.

Servings: 12
Prep Time: 10 Minutes
Cook Time: 20 Minutes

2 1/2 cups uncooked oatmeal
1 cup flour
2 eggs
1/2 teaspoon salt
1 cup butter
1 teaspoon vanilla
1 cup brown sugar
1/3 cup sugar
1 teaspoon baking soda
1 teaspoon ground cinnamon
1 cup raisins

1. Start by preheating your toaster oven to 350°F.
2. Mix together vanilla, brown sugar, butter, and salt.
3. Add sugar, eggs, baking soda, and cinnamon one at a time until fully mixed.
4. Stir in the oats, then stir in the raisins.
5. Drop spoonfuls of mixture onto an ungreased baking sheet (about six per batch).
6. Bake for 20 minutes.

Nutrition
Calories: 353, Sodium: 326 mg, Dietary Fiber: 2.6 g, Total Fat: 17.3 g, Total Carbs: 46.7 g, Protein: 4.8 g.

Cinnamon Apple Tart

This is a simple recipe for a simple dessert; sometimes the classics are the best.

Servings: 1
Prep Time: 10 Minutes
Cook Time: 15 Minutes

2 teaspoons light brown sugar
1/2 teaspoon ground cinnamon
1 (6-inch) flour tortilla
1 tablespoon unsalted butter
1/2 honey crisp apple
Salt to taste

1. Melt butter and slice apples into 1/8-inch-thick slices.
2. Mix together cinnamon and sugar.
3. Brush tortilla with butter and sprinkle with half the sugar and cinnamon.
4. Toast in a toaster oven until tortilla crisps, about 3 minutes.
5. Arrange the apple slices in a circle around the tortilla.
6. Return to toaster oven and toast for another 10 minutes.
7. Sprinkle with salt to taste.

Nutrition

Calories: 227, Sodium: 250 mg, Dietary Fiber: 4.3 g, Total Fat: 12.4 g, Total Carbs: 30.1 g, Protein: 1.8 g.

Blackberry Peach (or Apple) Cobbler

This is another take on the classic cobbler. Mixing tart blackberries with sweet peach makes your tongue want to dance.

Servings: 12
Prep Time: 25 Minutes
Cook Time: 30 Minutes

- 1 1/2 cups sliced peaches or apples
- 1 cup blackberries
- 3 tablespoons coconut sugar
- 1 1/2 teaspoons cinnamon
- 2 1/2 cups dry oats
- 1 egg
- 1/2 cup unsweetened applesauce
- 3/4 cups almond milk
- 1/2 cup chopped walnuts or hazel nuts
- 1 tablespoon coconut oil, melted
- 1/2 teaspoon cinnamon

1. Start by preheating the toaster oven to 350°F.
2. Combine peaches, berries, sugar, and 1 teaspoon cinnamon in a medium saucepan over medium heat. Simmer for about 20 minutes, stirring regularly.
3. While the peaches cook, beat egg in a large bowl, then mix in apple sauce and milk.
4. Put 2 cups oatmeal in a separate bowl and pour egg mixture over oatmeal.
5. Pour oatmeal into a greased baking pan and top with peach mixture.
6. Mix together coconut oil, walnuts, coconut sugar, and 1/2 teaspoon cinnamon, and pour over pan.
7. Bake for 30 minutes.

Nutrition

Calories: 176, Sodium: 9 mg, Dietary Fiber: 3.7 g, Total Fat: 9.4 g, Total Carbs: 20.6 g, Protein: 4.7 g.

Blueberry Cream Cheese Croissant Puff

This is one of my favorite desserts ever. It is so rich and creamy, and if it wasn't for my waistline, I would probably eat one every night.

Servings: 10
Prep Time: 30 Minutes
Cook Time: 40 Minutes

- 3 large croissants
- 1 cup fresh or frozen blueberries
- 1 package (8-ounce) cream cheese
- 2/3 cups sugar
- 2 eggs
- 1 teaspoon vanilla
- 1 cup milk

1. Start by preheating toaster oven to 350°F.
2. Tear up croissants into 2-inch chunks and place them in a square pan.
3. Sprinkle blueberries over croissant chunks.
4. In a medium bowl, mix cream cheese, sugar, eggs, and vanilla.
5. Slowly add in milk, mixing as you go.
6. Pour cream cheese mixture over the croissants and let stand for 20 minutes.
7. Bake for 40 minutes.

Nutrition
Calories: 140, Sodium: 97 mg, Dietary Fiber: 0.5 g, Total Fat: 5.8 g, Total Carbs: 20.0 g, Protein: 3.2 g.

Peanut Butter & Jelly Bars

Some genius was sitting in their kitchen one day and thought to themselves, "How could I make peanut butter and jelly better?" Then they came up with an idea similar to this one.

Servings: 8
Prep Time: 10 Minutes
Cook Time: 20 Minutes

1/2 cup whole wheat pastry flour
1/2 teaspoon baking powder
1/4 teaspoon salt
1 small banana
1/4 cup smooth peanut butter
3 tablespoons real maple syrup
2 teaspoons melted coconut oil
1/2 teaspoon pure vanilla extract
2 tablespoons chopped raw shelled peanuts
2 tablespoons raspberry preserves

1. Start by preheating the toaster oven to 350°F.
2. Mash banana.
3. Mix banana, syrup, oil, peanut butter, and vanilla in a bowl until thoroughly combined.
4. In a separate large bowl add flour, salt, and baking powder and combine using a fork.
5. Create a hole in the flour mix and pour in banana mix.
6. Sprinkle with nuts and stir for 2 minutes.
7. Pour batter into a bread loaf pan lined with parchment paper. Drop 1/2 teaspoonfuls of raspberry preserves over batter.
8. Bake for 20 minutes.
9. Allow to cool, then transfer using the parchment paper and cut.

Nutrition

Calories: 143, Sodium: 78 mg, Dietary Fiber: 1.8 g, Total Fat: 6.5 g, Total Carbs: 19.0 g, Protein: 3.5 g.

Peanut Butter Cookies

This recipe is awesome because it has all the deliciousness of traditional peanut butter cookies, but in a single serving batch.

Servings: 1
Prep Time: 10 Minutes
Cook Time: 10 Minutes

2 tablespoons flour
1 1/2 tablespoons peanut butter
1/16 teaspoon baking soda
Pinch of salt
1/4 teaspoon pure vanilla extract
1 1/2 tablespoons maple syrup
1 teaspoon applesauce

1. Start by pre-heating the toaster oven to 350°F.
2. Mix all of the dry ingredients together in one bowl.
3. Mix in peanut butter, then the rest of the ingredients.
4. Spray a small pan and drop cookies onto pan, then flatten.
5. Bake for 10 minutes.

Nutrition
Calories: 281, Sodium: 348 mg, Dietary Fiber: 1.9 g, Total Fat: 12.3 g, Total Carbs: 37.5 g, Protein: 7.6 g.

Cinnamon Pear
Oatmeal Crisp

Everyone loves delicious apple crisp, and I can't argue this, but it's been done. By replacing the apples with pears, you get a whole new flavor profile that livens up a classic.

Servings: 1
Prep Time: 10 Minutes
Cook Time: 25 Minutes

1 cup pears
2 tablespoons rolled oats
1 tablespoon whole wheat pastry flour
1 tablespoon brown sugar
1 tablespoon butter
1/2 teaspoon cinnamon
Fresh grated nutmeg to taste

1. Start by peeling and slicing the pear into thin slices, about 1 cup.
2. Preheat the toaster oven to 375°F.
3. Place the pears in an oven-safe dish.
4. In a separate bowl, mix together all other ingredients and pour on top of pears.
5. Bake for 25 minutes.

Nutrition
Calories: 300, Sodium: 87 mg, Dietary Fiber: 7.4 g, Total Fat: 12.7 g, Total Carbs: 46.9 g, Protein: 2.9 g.

Buttery Plum
Clafoutis

Some say it's a cobbler, others a custard, but no matter what you call it, it's 100% delicious.

Servings: 8
Prep Time: 10 Minutes
Cook Time: 45 Minutes

2 tablespoons unsalted butter
1 cup whole milk
1/3 cup granulated sugar
1/2 teaspoon grated nutmeg
1/4 teaspoon salt
3 eggs
1/2 cup whole wheat pastry flour
4 plums

1. Start by halving the plums and removing the pits.
2. Preheat the toaster oven to 400°F.
3. Melt butter in a large bowl and add in milk, sugar, nutmeg, salt, and eggs.
4. Spray an 8-inch-square baking sheet and pour batter in the pan.
5. Push plums, inside down, into the pan and bake for 45 minutes.

Nutrition
Calories: 137, Sodium: 129 mg, Dietary Fiber: 1.1 g, Total Fat: 5.7 g, Total Carbs: 17.9 g, Protein: 4.0 g.

Single-Serving Chocolate Chip Cookies

Okay, so this one really doesn't need an explanation. If you don't love chocolate chip cookies, then I need proof that you are a human being and not an alien.

Servings: 1
Prep Time: 10 Minutes
Cook Time: 8 Minutes

- 2 tablespoons butter
- 2 firmly packed tablespoons dark brown sugar
- 1 tablespoon granulated sugar
- Pinch of salt
- 1/4 teaspoon pure vanilla extract
- 1 egg yolk
- 1/4 teaspoon baking soda
- 1/4 cup all-purpose flour
- 3 heaping tablespoons semi-sweet chocolate chips

1. Start by preheating the toaster oven to 350°F.
2. Soften butter and combine with sugars, salt, and vanilla.
3. Add egg yolk and continue to stir.
4. Add flour and baking soda and stir until combined.
5. Add chocolate chips to the bowl and mix until evenly distributed.
6. Line a pan with parchment paper and separate dough into two equal parts in pan.
7. Bake for 8 minutes.

Nutrition

Calories: 667, Sodium: 645 mg, Dietary Fiber: 3.1 g, Total Fat: 39.9 g, Total Carbs: 73.4 g, Protein: 6.2 g.

Oatmeal Cookie Peach Cobbler

This dessert combines two favorites to create an entirely new flavor profile. It is a fun and tasty dessert that is perfect for a summertime get together.

Servings: 12
Prep Time: 40 Minutes
Cook Time: 40 Minutes

Topping:

1/2 cup granulated sugar
1/2 cup packed brown sugar
1/2 cup softened butter
2 teaspoons vanilla extract
1 large egg
1 cup all-purpose flour
1 cup old-fashioned rolled oats
1/2 teaspoon baking powder
1/2 teaspoon salt

Filling:

11 cups sliced peeled peaches
1/3 cup granulated sugar
2 tablespoons all-purpose flour
2 tablespoons fresh lemon juice

1. Start by preheating toaster oven to 350°F.
2. Combine butter and sugars in a medium bowl until creamed and set aside.
3. Add vanilla and egg and mix well.
4. Combine the flour, oats, and baking powder in a separate bowl.
5. Mix sugar mixture and flour mixture together.
6. Cover the bowl and refrigerate for half an hour.
7. While the topping chills, make the filling by combining peaches, lemon juice, flour, and sugar in a bowl.
8. Spray a baking dish with cooking spray and fill it with peach mix.
9. Dollop spoonfuls of the topping evenly over the peaches. Bake for 40 minutes.

Nutrition

Calories: 281, Sodium: 160 mg, Dietary Fiber: 3.4 g, Total Fat: 9.0 g, Total Carbs: 48.5 g, Protein: 4.2 g.

Strawberry Chocolate Chip Banana Bread Bars

The name really says it all. This dessert is not only relatively healthy, but it will easily become a standard in the household.

Servings: 10
Prep Time: 15 Minutes
Cook Time: 30 Minutes

- 1 1/4 cups white whole wheat flour
- 1 cup old-fashioned rolled oats
- 1 teaspoon ground cinnamon
- 1 1/2 teaspoons baking soda
- 2 bananas
- 1 egg
- 1/4 cup packed brown sugar
- 2 tablespoons melted coconut oil
- 3/4 cups + 1 tablespoon reduced-fat buttermilk
- 1 cup freeze-dried strawberries
- 1/4 cup semi-sweet mini chocolate chips

1. Start by preheating the toaster oven to 350°F.
2. Stir dry ingredients together in a medium bowl.
3. In a separate bowl, mash bananas and mix with egg, then add brown sugar, oil, and buttermilk.
4. Combine flour mixture with banana mixture. Fold in strawberries and chocolate chips.
5. Pour batter into a greased cake pan and bake for 30 minutes. Allow to cool then enjoy.

Nutrition

Calories: 187, Sodium: 220 mg, Dietary Fiber: 2.4 g, Total Fat: 5.4 g, Total Carbs: 31.1 g, Protein: 4.5 g.

www.ingramcontent.com/pod-product-compliance
Lightning Source LLC
Chambersburg PA
CBHW051805100526
44592CB00016B/2566